A Funny Thing Happened on the Way to the Trout Stream

Enjoy the Way to the Trout Stream!

Dave Pabst

A Funny Thing Happened on the Way to the Trout Stream
Forty Years Trout Fishing in Europe & North America

Dick Pobst

Acknowledgements

Copyright © 2011 by Dick Pobst
Published by Thornapple Angling Classics

Editor	*Elissa Curcio*
Computer design	*Ellis White*
Marketing	*Jake Pobst*
Design	*Rachael Pobst*
Advisors	*Howard Meyerson, Allen Jones, Dick Smith*
Permissions: Voelker Foundation	*Testament*

The author gratefully acknowledges the permission to quote the **Testament of a Fisherman** granted by the Voelker Family (Kitchie Hill, Inc.) which invites those who share the sentiments it expresses to consider supporting the work of the John D. Voelker Foundation. For information, visit the Foundation's website, Voelkerfdn.org.

Joanne Foote	*Autumn Float,* print © 1988 by Jim Foote
The Lyons Press	Excerpts from *Spring Creek* © 1992 by Nick Lyons and excerpts from *Hunting & Fishing from A to Zern* © 1985 by Ed Zern
Norris McDowell	*Photos of John Voelker*
ISBN	Ten Digit ISBN: 1461150558
	Thirteen Digit ISBN: 9781461150558

D EDICATION

T his book tells of the help I received from several prominent anglers and authors, but it is dedicated to my wife, Nancy, who was my full partner in the business of fly fishing. Her amazing talents in sales, finance and administration were indispensable.

I have worked with some excellent administrators in my spotted career, but none was more capable than Nancy. I could always count on her to have superb ideas about any project, and she was always positive about any job we had to do.

Very few men have ever had the benefit of such a capable partner in life.

TABLE OF CONTENTS

PREFACE: A LONG JOURNEY TO THE TROUT STREAM

A love of the outdoors hooked me when I was a little kid, brought up in rural Ohio, and a restless nature kept me on the move. It was not until I was in my thirties that I got interested in fly fishing for trout, and that has kept me fascinated into my early eighties.

I worked on farms as a kid in Ohio and later in Texas. I asked my farm boss if he would hire me when I got out of high school. He knew I had been offered a college scholarship, so he told me to take it and then see what I wanted to do. After college and the army I had the urge to work in international business, and that led me to assignments in South America, by that time with a family.

After returning to the United States, I stumbled into fly fishing for trout, which ultimately became a turning point. I pursued fishing as a hobby while continuing to work internationally.

When I started trout fishing I was exasperated by the constant snagging of my flies. I hit upon a way to make flies snagless, and they were patented and brought to market. This led to my writing magazine articles about the flies, which eventually led to writing fly-fishing books.

After twenty years in international business, traveling over most of what we then knew as the free world, I decided to go into the business of fly fishing. My wife and I started a fly-fishing shop in Grand Rapids, Michigan. This led to our being hired by the Orvis Company to develop a dealer organization in a five-state area, which provided many fascinating experiences helping people start new businesses.

It was a great privilege to get well acquainted with several major contributors to the development of fly fishing in the second half of the twentieth century. Among others, they included John Voelker, author of *Anatomy of a Murder*; Carl Richards, coauthor of *Selective Trout*; Leigh Perkins, owner of Orvis, and his sons, Perk and Dave; Nick Lyons, who published most of the fly-fishing books during that period; Ernie Schwiebert, author of *Matching the Hatch*; and Dermot Wilson, the great British angler.

I heard many amusing stories and saw a lot of funny, quaint signs on my fishing travels. I found that the farther from civilization you travel, the more creative signs become, in spelling, punctuation, and wording. They are a key part of this book. Sometimes signs were photographed in difficult conditions, but are included for the humor.

After forty-plus years trout fishing and doing business throughout the world, I am happy to be writing this memoir in retirement. I hope readers will get as much enjoyment from this recounting as I had in the experience.

The introduction, about Carl Richards, does not follow the chronological order of the book, but is so placed because it explains why I chose to specialize in fly fishing.

SPELLING AND PUNCTUATION GET MORE CREATIVE
THE CLOSER YOU GET TO A TROUT STREAM.

CARL RICHARDS ON THE RIVER TEST.

"Forget about the hundreds of flies—just concentrate
on the few most important hatches on your stream."
—Carl Richards

INTRODUCTION: CARL RICHARDS, MENTOR

Moving to Michigan exposed me to fly fishing for trout, and it was there where I learned about Carl Richards and his epic book, *Selective Trout*, which were to become the greatest influences on my fishing. I called Carl and went to his home near Grand Rapids sometime in the early 1970s. This was the beginning of a long friendship in which he taught me about the importance of fly hatches to trout fishing.

Selective Trout, which Carl wrote with Doug Swisher in 1971, was hailed as the most revolutionary approach to fly fishing in the twentieth century. It taught us numerous vital lessons and made fly fishing understandable to the average serious angler. I learned more from *Selective Trout* than from any other book, and I learned more from Carl Richards than from any other angler. Let's take a look at the lessons.

Lesson 1: Selectivity

The first lesson was that trout are selective. They become fussy when a fly hatch is on and tend to feed exclusively on flies that they have already found perfectly safe. Their protection against dying is their selectivity. It is hard to deceive trout—they are wary and have keen senses. The more they are feeding, the fussier they become. Carl and

6

Doug were not the first to realize this fact, but their book title alone shows the importance they gave it. The principle is that trout will feed exclusively on the hatch of insects that provides them with the most food with the least effort and the greatest safety. They will often continue to feed steadily on tiny midges and will not switch to much larger stoneflies until it is obvious to the nose on their snouts that there is a better meal to be had.

Lesson 2: Super Hatches
The next lesson was that in any river there are a few major hatches that provide the very best fishing. Carl and Doug called them the Super Hatches. When I was just starting to get serious about fly fishing, I asked Carl how to sort through the hundreds of artificial flies found in the catalogs. He told me to forget about the hundreds and concentrate on the few most important hatches of natural insects on the stream I fished, and find natural-looking patterns to imitate them. The Super Hatches vary from one river to another, but the major ones are similar in regions of the eastern United States, the Midwest, and the West.

Lesson 3: Pleasant Time of the Day
Carl and Doug taught us that the best hatches and the best fishing times occur at the pleasant time of the day. This is true in the spring when the fish are only active at the warmest time of day. It is true in the heat of summer when most activity only begins after the cool of the evening arrives. It is true during freezing winter days when insects and fish become most active as the rays of the sun are on the water. For that reason you can plan to fish at the times hatch activity is expected rather than fishing endless unproductive hours.

Lesson 4: Realistic Fly Patterns
Carl and Doug knew that most anglers often did poorly during major hatches. They reasoned it was because most flies used before 1970 were poor imitations of natural insects. Most fly-fishing writers

mention the no-hackle fly as Carl and Doug's major contribution, but that is only a small part of the broader lesson that artificial flies should resemble naturals. Most of the fly patterns that knowledgeable anglers use today were unknown in the old days, and older patterns have disappeared. Carl and Doug promoted lifelike imitations using not only the no-hackle fly but also the thorax tie, the hen spinner, the paradrake, the emerger, and other variations.

Carl's Influence on Fly Fishing

Before *Selective Trout* was published, Carl and Doug spent a lot of time teaching midwestern anglers, including members of Trout Unlimited, about the hatches. Al Caucci and Bob Nastase, authors of *Hatches*, and Art Flick, author of *Streamside Guide*, had done the same thing in the East. The influence of all these men was so great that one western fly shop owner told me that in the 1970s almost all the guides he hired were young men from Michigan, Pennsylvania, and New York. Nowadays there are plenty of excellent guides in the West, but at first many of them emigrated from the East and the Midwest.

Carl wrote or co-authored over a dozen books, mostly with Doug Swisher. The best known of these are probably *Fly Fishing Strategy* and *Emergers*. But undoubtedly his major work was *Selective Trout*, one of the best-selling fly-fishing books of the twentieth century and certainly the most influential in advancing the skills of fly fishermen. Doug moved west to be a guide before I moved to Grand Rapids.

Fishing with Carl, and More Lessons Learned

Carl developed a love for fishing as a boy. His mother died when he was young, and his father was a traveling salesman and golfer. Carl convinced his dad that since he was gone most of the time they should spend their summers near a trout stream. Therefore, during summer vacations, beginning when Carl was eight, they would frequently hang their hats near Michigan's Au Sable River. Carl could fish and camp out all he wanted while his father went golfing. During the school year Carl would tie flies for a local sports shop for spending money.

■ ■ ■ ■ ■

Carl and I both took Thursdays off to fish, and for several years we fished together regularly, driving to whichever river we thought might give us the best hatches. He soon had me convinced it was a lot more interesting fishing the hatches and spinner falls than flogging the stream all day. There is a lot greater chance of catching fish at those times.

The lessons Carl taught me were invaluable. After a few years, it got so I could contribute to his knowledge, although he still had the edge.

One night we sat by the fire at the Ginger Quill lodge on the Au Sable, chatting with some fishing friends about the behavior of spinners during the mating swarm and such. At 3:00 a.m. I noticed Carl and I were the only ones left awake. I told him we were obviously the only ones who gave a damn about that subject.

Another time, on one of my earliest trips to Michigan's Rogue River (this Rogue is a small river twenty minutes from my home, not to be confused with the famous Rogue River of Oregon) with Carl, I saw a dense swarm of flies in the air highlighted by the evening sun. I called it to his attention and he said, "Those are sulfur spinners. Tie on a spent wing fly because you are about to experience one of the best fishing events ever." We did, and had fish on almost continuously for nearly two hours.

■ ■ ■ ■ ■

Carl was a complete student of fishing. He had multiple aquariums to raise, study, and photograph aquatic insects. In the process he studied and taught himself aquatic entomology and macro photography. He spent countless hours observing, collecting, and photographing the insects.

Carl convinced me to put an aquarium in my basement to observe the behavior of flies. I rigged a video camera to run for three hours so we could tape the insects as they swam up in the water column and then hatched at the surface. I wanted to observe the giant *Hexagenia* mayflies hatching, so I went to the river and dug up

IF YOU DRIVE LIKE HELL, YOU WON'T FIGURE
OUT THE BOTTOM PART OF THE SIGN.

Carl and I occasionally drove down the road to Ma Deeter's for lunch and always got a kick out of her sign about driving like hell.

silt from the delta. I dumped it into the aquarium and proceeded to videotape the emergence.

Soon after, my wife Nancy noticed flies all over the house. I knew the probable cause but played dumb. Included in the silt had been numerous blowflies, which are similar to the housefly but much bigger. They were lumbering around all over the house. It took me a few days to swat all the darn things. Needless to say I did not repeat the experiment, but I had collected many feet of videotape that clearly showed how the insects emerged and hatched.

■ ■ ■ ■ ■

Carl's knowledge of the fly hatches was impressive. Of course, he knew all the scientific names which we simplistically call Latin names. One day Carl was telling my son Sam and me a story that included his three daughters, but he stumbled when it came to naming which of his daughters had done what. Sam asked, "Carl, why don't you give your daughters Latin names so you can remember them?"

■ ■ ■ ■ ■

Carl got in trouble when he decided to experiment with scented flies and wrote about it in one of the magazines. He drew a scathing attack from the leader of a conservation organization who wrote in a letter to the editor that Carl should be drummed out of the corps for using unsporting methods. Carl took it personally and was tempted to write a nasty letter in return. We discussed it and finally settled on a less contentious approach. We composed a letter saying this experiment had been done in the interest of science and that the scented flies had proven so effective they should be outlawed! Carl was a hero, and the conservationists were vindicated.

■ ■ ■ ■ ■

Carl and I used to fish on the Muskegon River at a place known as Carmichael Flats. We knew the river was prime habitat for caddisflies and sometimes had good fishing, but we didn't really understand the caddis—that came much later.

There is still good fishing there, but the directions have changed. Originally, you had to go north on Thornapple Road to the mailbox full of bullet holes, go right on the two-track to the Boy Scout observation tower, then go down the bank to the island, and that was Carmichael Flats. Now you still go north on Thornapple Road, as before, to where there *used to be* a mailbox full of bullet holes, and go right on the two-track. You then go east to where the two-track *used to go*, and follow the path to where there *used to be* a Boy Scout observation tower. Then you head down the bank to where there *used to be* an island, and that is Carmichael Flats. Good fishing, if you can get there.

■ ■ ■ ■ ■

It took several years to fully understand caddisflies, but Carl and I had enough good evenings of fishing to keep us coming back to the chase.

Among the things we learned was the fact that we could ignore the 193 species of caddis listed in Gary LaFontaine's *Caddisflies* and work with a handful of patterns. Also, we found that the caddisflies do not rocket out of the water upon emerging. They slowly breaststroke to the surface, and then drift slowly as pupae attached to the surface film, which makes floating pupae by far the most important fly pattern during emergence. Carl and I ended up writing a whole book on the subject, *The Caddisfly Handbook.*

THE OWNER WAS HAPPY TO POSE BY HIS SIGN.

Carl and I both did a double take when we came around a
corner on the way to the Jordan River and saw this sign on
the Harley shop.

Endings

Carl and I drifted apart as we got older. We fished less, and read and spent more time with our families. I was surprised when his wife, Alecia, called and said Carl was in hospice. I drove to the hospital and found him in a weakened state. It was springtime, and I asked him if he wanted to drive out to the river. "I want to. But can I?" was his response.

Carl died in 2006, on Memorial Day. The rock memorial erected by Trout Unlimited is an understated tribute, highly appropriate for the modest guy who was a major contributor to the fly-fishing world. The memorial read:

Carl Edward Richards
1933–2006
In memory of Dr. Carl Richards
His innovative and scientific approach
to angling changed fly fishing
forever.

THE APOSTROPHES ARE A SURE SIGN OF THE NORTH
COUNTRY, BUT THE SPELLING IS DAN QUAYLE'S.

PART I: Childhood & First Jobs, 1931–1963

1 AN OUTDOOR KID

I was born in 1931 in the depths of the Great Depression. As a kid I always wanted to be outdoors. When we lived in the city there were parks to explore. When we lived in the country I had woods, creeks, hills, and caves to enjoy.

Small-Town College Life

In 1938, when I was eight years old, my dad was named president of a tiny college, Rio Grande College, in southeastern Ohio. My brother, sister, and I were not really aware of what the Depression was like for most people, as our family was fairly well off. I later was amazed to read a clipping from the *Columbus Dispatch* saying my dad was the youngest college president in the state, with a princely salary of $5,000 a year. Haircuts cost 25 cents, and the old barber's scissors were dull and hurt with every cut. A bag of candy cost 10 cents, my weekly allowance. Our school had four rooms for six grades.

The town of Rio Grande was in a very poor part of the state, in the foothills of Appalachia. Most people there were farmers or coal miners. My family had electricity, but a lot of my friends did not. Jack, one of my best friends, lived in a log house. To get to it I crossed a log bridge across the "crick." Their home was lit by kerosene lanterns. The family burned coal dug from the hillside for heat and cooking. Jack's mother made dresses out of feed sacks printed with flower patterns. His father had a factory job in town and brought home essentials like salt, ammunition, coffee, overalls, shoes—and not much else. They grew their own vegetables, fruit, and meat, and kept a cow for milk, eventually to be butchered for meat. I loved it there. It was always a happy household. They were as cheerful and friendly as people could be, and Jack was my kind of guy. He was game for any expedition I could come up with.

Rio Grande College was called a "self-help" school. Students from this poor hill country were not permitted to pay for their room, board, or tuition; instead, they had to work their way through school. The girls lived in a dorm and worked in the college canning plant or cafeteria, or they cleaned the buildings. Most of the boys lived and worked on the college farm, staying in a house they named Alcatraz. They cooked their own meals, mostly in a cast-iron skillet on top of a potbellied coal stove.

I frequently stopped by Alcatraz for breakfast after I had checked my trap line on the farm. I caught 'possums and 'coons, and once I caught a black skunk. The college boys were "cool" guys from the hills, descended from early Anglo settlers, with names like Jack Duncan and Virgil McNulty, two I remember most.

Southern Ohio is basketball country, mainly because it only takes five guys to make a team, compared to eleven for football or nine for baseball. Rio Grande College was best known for its perennial championship basketball team, playing small colleges from Ohio, West Virginia, Kentucky, and Michigan. Jack Duncan scored 88 points in one game, an NCAA record at that time. Bevo Francis, also of Rio Grande, later outdid him with 113 points in a single game. The football team was different, having gone many years without scoring a touchdown. Eventually they made the *New York Times* sports page for scoring one touchdown in a game. They still lost by a big score. I think that was 1940. After Pearl Harbor all the fit players, who had been in a naval version of ROTC called V12, were activated, and the football team got even worse.

My family lived in the college president's house on a ten-acre apple orchard. At cider time I liked lying open-mouthed under the spigot of the cider press. Just down the road was the college farm, where I loved to hang out and work. My friends and I worked for $10 a month, hoeing corn and vegetables, shocking wheat, and pitching hay. The college boys milked the cows by hand, and the milk was delivered to the community in metal buckets with lids, earning income for the school.

Horses were originally used for farm work. Hay was cut with a horse-drawn mower, dried then pitchforked onto wagons, and hauled to the barns. Wheat was cut with a McCormack binder that mowed the straw, which was then tied into sheaves. We piled the sheaves into shocks and later pitched the sheaves into a threshing machine run by a steam engine, which towed the threshing machine from farm to farm. Local farmers all worked together at threshing time. Farm wives gathered to feed the hungry men three times a day. When the work was done on one farm, everyone moved the operation to the next.

My dad and the farm manager made the college farm more productive by introducing tractors, trucks, combines, corn pickers, milking machines, and even a pasteurizing plant that made cottage cheese and bottled the milk so it could be sold in bottles instead of buckets.

We kids worked as a group at all the jobs, and took pride in the fact that our gang could keep up with the college boys. After they went into the service, we kept up with the men imported from Kentucky for the "war effort." As the young college men went to war the government brought in groups of workers from deep in Appalachia to work on farms. The workers from the hills were ineligible for the draft because of age or illiteracy. The government issued each an army blanket and a pair of overshoes.

When butchering hogs the farm manager would hire local farm wives to work in the kitchen of the big house making sausage. Skillets of bulk sausage cooked all day long, and we all helped ourselves. The farmhouse, by the way, is the brick building that appears in Bob Evans TV commercials and on package labels. Bob Evans bought the college farm sometime after we moved away.

The farm also had a twenty-acre vegetable garden. We all hated being assigned to work there because it was hot, sweaty work and there was little breeze in the rows between the vegetables.

We played, too. From age eight to twelve my buddies and I built rafts on nearby Raccoon Creek. We hid canned "supplies" in Daniel Boone's cave, about three miles from home. (Boone was widely believed to have spent nights in the caves that were common in the area.) We built crude log cabins in the woods, and requisitioned turnips and sweet corn from the garden and eggs from the hen houses. We sometimes rode the farm horses, but they just plodded along. We preferred riding ponies when we could—at least they would run at times. One of my buddies had a buck sheep, or ram, that would chase us and butt us off our feet if it could catch us. It was a fun game to get the buck to chase us down the path.

After the attack on Pearl Harbor in December 1941 we played war games. Being good patriots, we hid dynamite in the caves. That way we could blast the cliff and block the road if the Nazis tried to pass through the Ohio hills. I checked the attic of our home to see if my father kept a secret radio, since he had a German name, but there was no radio. We kids saved our meager pay to buy 10-cent defense stamps to be converted into war bonds. We heard a lot from the adults about rationing, but being farm kids we always had enough to eat.

Fortunately for me, my parents were content to let me roam at my discretion. Maybe it was easier than coping with my restlessness.

* * * * *

When I was twelve, we moved to Cleveland, where my dad had taken an administrative job. I got on my mother's nerves during spring vacation. I guess that was why she asked, "How would you like to hitchhike to see your grandparents?" They lived about 250 miles away, in Cincinnati. I was out the door in a few minutes. When my dad came home, he called my grandfather and had me put on the next bus home. That summer my parents found a job for me at my aunt's restaurant, also about 250 miles away, which seemed like a comfortable distance. I never spent a summer at home again. We had a happy family, but I thrived being more or less on my own, and my family realized it.

Malabar Farm

My dad was a member of an early conservation organization called Friends of the Land, which was dedicated to promoting conservation on farms. One year he took me along to a Friends directors' meeting at Malabar Farm near Mansfield, Ohio. Malabar was the home of author Louis Bromfield, and it was where Bromfield's good friends Humphrey Bogart and Lauren Bacall were married.

Bromfield wrote thirty books, all best sellers. *Early Autumn* won the Pulitzer Prize, and some of his books, such as *The Rains Came* and *Mrs. Parkington*, were made into successful motion pictures. He served with the American Ambulance Service in World War I and was twice decorated. After living in France and India, he returned to the United States in 1939, turned to nonfiction, and became a leading advocate of modern farming and conservation practices.

For some reason, I caught Bromfield's attention. He knew I had experience working on the college farm and asked if I'd like to spend my summers working at Malabar, where they always had four or five boys employed. So that is what I did during the summers of '46, '47, and '48, starting when I was fourteen. We boys worked hard, and played hard. We could always use the farm jeep or truck if we wanted to go to town, where the merchants sponsored free outdoor movies on Saturday nights and an occasional square dance open to the public. I had a restricted driver's license that I used unrestrictedly.

The Ohio hills were gently rolling, with hardwood trees where it was too steep to farm. Although farming had depleted some of the land, the underlying limestone made it possible to restore the soil, which Bromfield realized. So on a farm, you would have pastures, field crops, hardwoods such as maples that provided gorgeous red and yellow colors in the fall and maple sugar in the spring, and caves in the woods that amused the kids.

There were five farmhouses on the farm, not counting Bromfield's Big House. We kids lived in one of the farmhouses, where we usually took our meals. We were always welcome at the Big House, though, even for meals. If there was room, we could eat at the table with the Bromfields. If not, we would eat in the little dining room reserved for the household help.

Ordinarily the dairyman's wife fed us. I once saw Harry the dairyman get mad at a cow and knock it to its knees with a fist to the head. No one trifled with Harry. Harry's house had an old stone springhouse, which served as a cooler. We'd get a drink there on hot days, and swim and bathe in the farm pond across the road.

I was handy with machinery, so after the first year they put me in charge of the tractor-mounted mowing machine. It was my job to mow the hay and straw, to keep the rig in repair, and in my spare time to mow the pastures to keep down weeds. I particularly loved to mow one large pasture that was up a long lane on top of a hill surrounded by woods. I'd go there evenings to mow and to enjoy the cool evening air and pretty rolling pasture, and often watched red foxes running through the green fields.

Louie Bromfield was very interested in us kids. He would talk to us about farming any time we wanted. One day while Louie was talking to another boy and me on the porch, his secretary, George, came out to tell him that the U.S. Secretary of Agriculture needed attention indoors. Louie told George to tell him he was busy with the boys and he'd be in later.

Louie and George were avid opera fans. After a few drinks they would sometimes perform *La Traviata*, their favorite. I don't know if they were any good, but Louie would get our attention when he stood on a sofa to sing. He was a rugged-looking man, over six feet tall and deeply tanned, with a wrinkled face and a gray crew cut, and usually a cigarette dangling from his lips. We called him "Mr. B," and he introduced me to fishing. We would pile in his big Buick station wagon on summer evenings and go to a nearby lake to catch milk buckets full of bluegills to stock the pond so he and his guests could fish in it. That was well before my fly-fishing days. We fished with worms dangled from bamboo poles.

"Git You Yankees"

In 1949, when I was seventeen, Bromfield's farm manager sent my pal Zeke and me to Texas to start up a new farm project, reclaiming depleted land. The project was sponsored by the Chamber of Commerce of Wichita Falls, 125 miles northwest of Dallas. They wanted to use Bromfield's updated farming methods to rejuvenate some badly misused farmland. The land had been made unproductive by earlier farming methods, which only plowed four or five inches deep, creating a deep, hard pan that would not hold water. The farming methods of the times were one of the causes of the Dust Bowl. The soil was further damaged by saltwater runoff from the nearby oil wells.

Zeke and I lived in a house on the farm, about two miles from a small town called KMA, which was once an oil boomtown. It was twenty miles from Wichita Falls, the nearest city with movies and such attractions. The town was named KMA because it was at the juncture of three ranches owned by the Kemp, Munger, and Allen families. The mapmakers called it Kamay. The population declined to about one hundred people after the oil boom.

We befriended a young, soft-spoken Texan named Hank, who had just finished a hitch in the U.S. Marines. He had no car and he needed transportation. We had a Jeep and we needed a local guide. We formed a team.

Hank's father, Woodrow, claimed that Jesse James shot his brother. Woodrow said he confronted Jesse, saying, "Jess, you shot my brother." Jesse, as the story went, said, "I had to, Woody, he drew on me." Woody responded, "Well, I understand, Jess." End of story. It didn't pay to push Jesse too hard.

Zeke and I took our meals at a small cafe in town. One day

when Hank was eating with us, a waitress at the cafe whispered to me, "Dick, them boys from the pool hall are fixin' to git you Yankees." I thanked her and we steered clear of the pool hall. Nothing happened to us, so after a few weeks I asked the waitress about it. She seemed amazed. "You ain't heard? Well, the day after I told you about it your friend Hank walked into the pool hall. He grabbed a cue off'n the rack and broke it over the edge of a table. That got their attention. Then he said, soft like he talks, 'I heered you boys was fixin' to git my Yankee friends. If ya do, I'm gonna kill ya!'"

It pays to have friends in low places, especially one who speaks softly and carries a splintered stick.

NEVER BE LEF'D.

2 OFF TO PANAMA

I met my wife, Nancy, in high school. We were married right after college. We graduated in 1953 and the army drafted me that same year. I spent two years at Fort Lewis, Washington. The truce had been reached in Korea, and we were strictly in training. After basic training we were allowed weekend passes. Nancy drove from Michigan to Washington, where we rented an apartment in the state capital of Olympia.

After our son, Sam, was born in 1954, we rented a two-room house. We could see Puget Sound and the snowcapped Olympic Mountains from the living room window, and Mount Rainier from the side window.

After the army I attended the Thunderbird School of International Management, where I took business and language classes. The company recruiters who came to campus were only offering around $200-a-month salaries, so I went on the road to find a job. One of my first interviews was with the international grain broker, Cargill. The interviewer said, "Making staff sergeant as a draftee was pretty good. How did you like the army?" Well, I didn't, and I said so in no uncertain terms. He thanked me and ushered me out the door. He had just retired from the army as a lieutenant general, and I doubt that he appreciated my attitude. I did not get an offer from him.

My next interview was with Caterpillar Tractor Co. of Peoria, Illinois, in 1956. Caterpillar was, and still is, an amazingly good company. I was hired and worked in the International Finance department for a few years, handling shipping and documentation of heavy machinery to South America. While we were in Peoria our daughter Amy was born.

Life in Panama

Caterpillar sent me to Panama as office supervisor in 1959. I developed a program working with Central American dealers on financial management and negotiated sales and financing arrangements with contractors.

Caterpillar had an excellent worldwide dealer organization. One of the company's presidents had said that they wanted their dealers to prosper, and their dealers' sons, and the sons' sons. Each dealership was organized into departments: sales, finance, parts, and service. Caterpillar's supporting field staff was organized the same way. So was the parent company, which also had manufacturing and research departments. We were there to help the dealers in every possible constructive way. It was a great business education. The dealer organization was only one reason Caterpillar was first in their industry. Excellence in product design, manufacturing, finance, and sales, and depth in management were others.

Although the Caterpillar office was located in Panama City, much of our business was in the Canal Zone. At that time Panama Canal authorities were engaged in substantially widening the canal. We loved Panama City, but the atmosphere in the Zone was like an army base, only worse. It looked like an army base but the American Canal Zone authorities practiced racial segregation, with separate water fountains, separate theaters, separate everything—pure Jim Crow. This caused a terrific strain on relations with the Panamanians. All Panamanian workers were subject to segregation, even the Caucasian Panamanians. I don't know what the authorities thought the

Panamanians would do to their water fountains. This was just a small part of what caused the troubles, but that's another story. We did take advantage of one benefit of the Canal: We were able to join the Fort Amador officers' club, which had a shark fence across a small bay so we could swim there safely.

While we were aware of the tensions caused by the Canal Zone, we were also aware that the Zone was in most respects the best employer of a good portion of the Panamanian population. Their wages and working conditions were much better than those of any local company. But there was constant tension, not only between the Americans and the Panamanians, but also between the Panamanians and the English-speaking West Indian workers imported to work in the Zone.

My wife Nancy gave me a spinning rod and reel, which was put to use fishing off the causeway at the entrance to the Panama Canal with a neighbor. With a casting range of fifty feet or so you couldn't cover much of the Pacific Ocean, so we didn't catch many fish. Once a year the trade winds reached Panama for a couple of months, from December to February. The wind blew the warm surface water out to sea, and colder water came up to the surface. This brought huge schools of baitfish and predators to the top. We caught mackerel and jack crevalle and occasionally caught corvina. That provided a lot of action, so I began to think there might be some merit to fishing. It was a step up from the Malabar Farm bluegills. Those ocean fish fought harder than bluegills and were lots more fun to catch.

A Trip into the Jungle

After we had been in Panama nearly a year a friend asked me to accompany an expedition into the Darien, a stretch of jungle between Panama City and Colombia. It was the last gap in the Pan-American Highway and the trip was in preparation for completing the highway. We traveled in dugout canoes with outboard motors up the Bayano River, which runs parallel to the ocean shore between a couple of mountain ranges.

We were mostly on the dry side of the isthmus so the jungle vegetation was not high. It was composed of low plants, including banana and mango trees. The dry season only lasted two months, from mid-December to mid-February when the trade winds blew. The temperature usually got into the nineties and it was humid the other ten months of the year. We were dripping with sweat during the day.

Within an hour after leaving the last Spanish-speaking town, we got into territory inhabited by two Indian tribes, the Chocos and the Cunas. They lived in separate villages near each other but did not mix. The Chocos wore only breechclouts (a cloth worn around the buttocks, says *Webster's*), but Cuna women wore elaborate clothing that incorporated colorful appliquéd fabric called *molas*. Each thought the other tribe was dirty—the Chocos because they did not wear clothes to keep the dirt off, and the Cunas because they wore clothes and the rain could not wash them clean.

The tribes spoke no English or Spanish, only Choco and Chibchan, but each village had a "secretary", or translator, who had been sent to Panama City to learn Spanish. We had to get permission from the village chiefs to proceed into their territory and to spend our nights there, sleeping in hammocks slung in thatched huts on their "plantations," where they went to gather fruits and bananas. It cost us a few cigarettes and some candy to gain entrance to their territory, and the process had to be repeated at each village. Once while negotiating entrance I asked the secretary the name of his chief. He wrote on a notebook: "Sonny Briggs." No one knew how he got the name, and no one remembered there ever being other English-speaking people in the village.

Night was when malaria-carrying mosquitoes were at large. Before dark, we would get into our mosquito-netted hammocks. Little of the cool evening air got through the netting and each night we tried to sleep in those hot hammocks while being serenaded by howler monkeys.

Our expedition was made strange by the inclusion of two rowdy Australians. One of their antics included shouting, as we approached a Choco village, "Despoilers of women and children!" Of course, no one could understand them and there was no substance to their charges, but it seemed to me a strange way to approach people from whom we were begging access and shelter.

Law School

I enrolled in the law school at the University of Panama, mainly to improve my Spanish. After my first exam, Nancy asked me how it went. One question was to describe the "hierarchical order of good." I told her I didn't understand what that meant in English, let alone Spanish.

This was around 1959, shortly after Castro took over Cuba. Communist-leaning students had taken over the university's central board. The board was organized so the administration had 25 percent of the votes, the teaching faculty had 25 percent, and the students had 50 percent. The communists controlled the students' vote so they and one professor could control the university. With this power, they used university funds to send students to Cuba for training with the intention of spreading the revolution in Latin America.

While we were there, the Cubans invaded Panama with about a hundred troops. They expected the Panamanians to rise up and support them—they didn't. That invasion created a backlash and the Panamanians kicked the Cubans out.

Being blond, in a country where 80 percent of the people were a mixture of Spanish and Indian, I stood out like a sore thumb. That made me a *rabiblanco*, or "whiteass." I became friends with the president of the students' group at the law school, a Czech refugee named Juan Castulovich. He and his four brothers—all ardent anti-communists—had fled Europe when the Russians invaded after World War II and moved to Panama.

One afternoon one of the students made a political speech stating, "We are going to kill all the blondes from Nova Scotia to Tierra del Fuego." Afterward the speaker came up to me and said, "This is nothing personal, Ricardo." I told him it was personal to me. A group of his friends gathered around and started arguing with me. Juan Castulovich came in and told them to leave me alone. They turned on him and threatened him. He said, "Look, we are five brothers and we have a pact. We have a list with all your names. If anything happens to any of us, we are going to get you (finger pointing), and you, and you . . ."

Another friend, an Italian immigrant named Gustavo Rosania, took special delight in walking into communist regional offices, over-turning tables, and throwing their pamphlets out into the streets. He and many others were responsible for the resistance that effectively drove the communists out of the country or underground.

One morning, newspaper headlines announced that Margot Fonteyn, prima ballerina of the British Royal Ballet, and her husband, Roberto "Tito" Arias, had been captured when they landed on a beach near Panama City trying to invade the country and topple the government, evidently with Cuban support. Why on earth would the great ballerina do this? No one knows for sure, but Tito had been president of Panama and apparently wanted to rule again. He hired a bunch of men and six sixty-foot shrimp boats and tried to get something started. The Guardia Nacional jailed Tito, and Dame Margot was exiled to England. Headlines like this provided amusement and such events seldom progressed any further.

The Confidence Man

An important Caterpillar customer lived right across the street from us in Panama City. His name was Rafael, and he had road-building contracts throughout Central America. I began to notice that wherever he had contracts local officials were getting arrested and jailed and the projects were going bankrupt. Rafael, however, always paid Caterpillar.

Later, in Argentina, Rafael's pattern of actions came back to haunt me. He told me he was born on a farm in eastern Cuba adjacent to the farm where Fidel Castro lived, and that his first wife was Fidel's sister. There were rumors he was funding Castro's revolutionary activities. He turned out to be the first con man I had ever met and I would meet him again, all too soon. I learned that capable con men often exhibit two characteristics: apparent honesty, and apparent sincerity. Deep down they seem to believe they are too smart to get caught.

COMPLAINTS ABOUT THE HOURLY RATES?

3 ON TO ARGENTINA

In 1961 Caterpillar sent me to Buenos Aires, Argentina—one of the world's most beautiful cities. Buenos Aires has much of the atmosphere of Paris. It has a moderate climate, tree-lined streets, spacious parks and broad avenues, sidewalk cafes, and barbecue stands lining the walk along the Rio de la Plata, an estuary too wide to see across. Nancy and I enjoyed seeing and hearing the stars of the European ballets and operas when they came to the lavish Colon opera house. Our kids learned to ride their bikes in the extensive parks that bordered the river. We had a great life living in a downtown apartment and I had bigger business challenges than in Panama.

There were five of us Americans there to assist the dealership whose business had fallen off dramatically. They were down to about 15 percent market share and in serious trouble. The dealership was owned by two Swedish families, and they were receptive to our help. Our strategy called for our engineers to help plan jobs for contractors while I negotiated financing. Our parts and service people made arrangements to facilitate repairs. We didn't waste time bidding on low-profit government jobs that were typically bid at cost—we were happy to let our competitors lose time and money on those. Our dealer was back up well over 50 percent market share in two years.

Life in Argentina

We lived through thirteen riots or revolutions in Latin America. Most had little effect on us, though I observed gunfire on a few occasions. During the worst uprisings businesses would close down. They would roll down and lock their heavy shutters and we would stay home. At one point two factions of the armed forces, the blue force and the red force, got into a fight. Nancy and the kids were forced off a train when the red force blockaded the railroad tracks. They were upset and scared when they felt the effects of drifting teargas. We spent one afternoon playing bridge and watching the blue air force dive-bomb the position of the red force at the railroad station across town.

We did not own a car, since the streetcars ran everywhere and cost a few pennies, and a taxi ride from my office to our apartment was just 15 cents. The apartment faced a pretty park with a huge spreading ombu tree. Ombus look something like the massive ever-green live oak trees of the southern United States, but they have large root structures above the ground.

The weather was seldom hot in the summer, except before a pampero, which is a sudden, cool windy storm that blows in off the pampas after a stifling heat wave. On the coldest days of winter there would occasionally be a skim of ice on some of the puddles in the morning. It was normally a beautiful and sunny place.

The predominant language is Spanish but the Italians strongly influence the inflections and food, especially in Buenos Aires. There are also many British immigrants, called Anglo-Argentines, and several have their own schools and businesses. Our daughter Amy was four when we lived in Buenos Aires and went to a British school. She came home the first day and said it was funny that even though they spoke another language (British), she could understand them.

The Caterpillar office was in a building that housed the Swedish consulate, the Swedish Club, and our dealership that was owned by two Swedish families. We could have a nice lunch in the club, but if we ate with the Swedes, we would be plied with aquavit (vodka). That could make you sleepy in the afternoon. Argentine workers on the streets outside would typically build a fire on the sidewalk to cook a steak, which they would wash down with a liter of red wine.

I frequently run into interesting people. In Buenos Aires one day, while waiting for a client in a hotel lobby, I spied a bull of a man who was having trouble with the clerks at the desk. I recognized him instantly: He was Primo Carnera, former world heavyweight boxing and wrestling champion. I would guess he weighed over three hundred pounds and it was not fat. When I introduced myself and we shook hands, his hand enveloped mine. He didn't speak Spanish so I offered to help. We quickly solved the problem he was having with his hotel reservation. I asked if he had been to Buenos Aires before and he boomed, "Yeah, about twenty-five years ago, and they haven't done a goddamn thing since then!" I arranged for him to visit a gaucho nightclub and wished him well.

The Andes

Our family usually spent our vacations in the United States, but felt we should get to know more of Argentina. So, in the winter of 1961, we decided to go to Bariloche in the Andes, where the kids and I got to enjoy skiing for the first time. The Andes are the highest mountains in the Western Hemisphere, and are impressively snow-covered all year long. The highest peak, Mount Aconcagua, is 23,000 feet tall and it was visible as the plane approached the airport.

The crew of the DC3 that flew us there was pretty casual. They invited our two kids, then ages five and seven, into the cockpit while Nancy and I remained in the cabin. Things were quiet for a little while, but then the plane started to bank right and left. It went up and down and the wing lights turned on and off. The kids came back excited. They said they had helped fly the plane, and that they had talked to the control tower and sang them "Oh My Darling, Clementine."

Gauchos

Gauchos are the cowboys of South America, and their old culture still existed when we were there. Like the Cossacks, their fellow horsemen of Russia, they engage in wild dancing, jumping high in the air and stomping the floor with their boots. The boots are high, pull-on types, and the tops are pleated, like an accordion, for flexibility. They wear baggy pants held up by sashes and tucked into their boots. Knives are stuck in the back of their sashes, and they use them to cut meat from a spit over a fire, holding one end of the meat chunk in a hand and the other end between the teeth, and then cutting off a piece to chew. Gauchos enjoy singing and declaiming poetry in the evenings. They drink yerba maté, an indigenous tea, when on the pampas or wine if they are near a source.

I have always liked rodeos and I never saw better riding than in Argentina. There I saw a remarkable rodeo, which they call a *doma*. In the *doma* they ride broncos both saddled and bareback. That day a gaucho jumped onto the judges' stand, which was a hay wagon, and grabbed the microphone. He was reputed to be the best rider and had been assigned the toughest bronc to ride bareback. "This horse had better run and jump and buck, because I am going to ride him until he stops," he announced over the speaker. It happened exactly as he said.

Pato is a game played by gauchos. Originally, it entailed mounted gauchos racing to the center of a field to grab a duck by the neck. The goal was to throw the duck into a four-foot circular net at the opponents' end of the field. When two opposing gauchos grabbed the same duck by the neck it tended to end the duck and therefore the game. Nowadays, they play with a soccer ball with handles taped onto it. It is hard on the shoulders of the rider who gets yanked off his horse, but fun is fun.

Rafael Returns

My old neighbor Rafael from Panama showed up in Buenos Aires trying to negotiate road-building contracts with several of the Argentine provinces. He wanted to buy machinery from Caterpillar and have us accept the notes or securities from the provinces directly as payment for the machinery without any obligation on his part. I was suspicious of what he was up to. It appeared to me that he could milk the construction income and leave us holding worthless notes.

I decided to investigate Rafael's activities and started traveling to the capitals of the provinces involved. I found that in every case there was evidence that provincial documents were forged or did not have the underlying legal authorization they claimed to have. Graft was behind every deal. Our chief engineer and I invited Rafael to lunch and told him we would not be able to accept the notes. Rafael threatened to get me fired but he backed down when I showed him the report I had filed exposing the graft. He stormed out of the restaurant, and I never heard from him again.

I recalled the rumors that Rafael might be bankrolling Fidel Castro's efforts to spread the revolution and I thought they were true. I reported my suspicions to our embassy officials.

NOT A MISSPELLING!
NO, THEIR YAPPING BESPOKE TERRORS.

PART II: Fly Fishing, 1963–1975

4 RETURN TO THE UNITED STATES

My experiences in Panama and Argentina were worthwhile, but I concluded I needed more than just Latin American experience to pursue my international career.

Aeroquip

Both Nancy's and my parents lived in Michigan so we had a place to stay when we returned to the United States in 1963. We were basically freeloading while I hunted for a job, interviewing at all the big companies that were seeking people with my background.

Nancy and my mother suggested I call on Aeroquip Corporation in Jackson, Michigan. Aeroquip was a medium-size Fortune 500 manufacturer of hydraulic hose lines and components. I thought it was a waste of time to call on Aeroquip, as there was no indication they were hiring, but just to satisfy my wife and mother, I knocked on the door of the president's home on a Sunday afternoon. I told him I was looking for an international job. He said he had just been thinking that they needed such a person and asked me to come to the Aeroquip offices for an interview.

The interview went well the next day at their headquarters. It was a great fit. They had significant overseas dealerships, licensees, and subsidiaries, but had not needed anyone to coordinate things until that time. So I started traveling the world, first to get acquainted with their operations, then to start developing new overseas businesses.

My job with Aeroquip was rewarding in that I not only traveled the free world but also had the responsibility of establishing manufacturing plants and acquiring subsidiaries, as well as developing dealerships. This turned out to be excellent experience which paid off later in the fly-fishing business.

Our third child, Andrea, was born in Jackson. That day I was fishing some thirty miles from home when I got the urgent call to shag it home. We made it to the hospital with only minutes to spare.

The Nazi

Around 1966 I met my second con man. He was the manager of our subsidiary in Germany, and ran a good operation. He was big-bellied, energetic, smart, aggressive, and he could be very charming. He hired and trained competent staff and the company he ran was efficient and profitable. I think that was why most of us accepted him despite the fact he was a former colonel in the Nazi SS.

To hear "the Colonel" tell it, he was nice to all the enemies of the Third Reich. He claimed he had rescued many Jews from his Nazi colleagues, but he had a sneering way of telling his stories—he made the Jews sound pathetic and stupid, even as he bragged about saving them. Interestingly enough, our wives were not fooled. Several of them were suspicious of him from the beginning.

The Colonel was often in trouble but could talk his way out of anything. He had the con man's apparent sincerity. He ran a very efficient company, but he was milking it for his own use. He was the king of his small town. Every time we thought we had the goods on him he would talk his way out of it. For example, he had built his home with company funds, but managed to cover his tracks for several years. He would threaten one of our licensees with cancellation and then deny it. He would admit he had said something but explain that the word in German also means something else, which was what he meant. Our company president was German born and educated, but the Colonel could often even fool him.

Our financial vice president went to Germany to confront the Colonel about some irregularities. One night after dinner, while the VP was unlocking his car, he was arrested and spent the night in jail charged with drunk driving. Somehow, no one could reach the Colonel until the next day despite the fact that he was sitting at home in the small town where everyone knew him. He made it clear that you should not come to his town and hassle him.

We finally caught the Colonel taking funds and fired him. Then we found out the German tax authorities were after him. They did not get him in time, however. One night he came home drunk and started a fight with his wife. She locked herself in her room, and he threatened to break the door down. His wife shot through the door and killed him as he tried to break in. She was, thank goodness, acquitted.

※ ※ ※ ※ ※

Aeroquip's international business grew and prospered during the eight years I was with them in Jackson. Eventually, we had subsidiaries in England, Germany, Brazil, and Canada; joint ventures in Japan and Mexico; and licensees in Spain, Italy, France, Argentina, Australia, and Scotland. But that was about to end.

Toledo

Around 1971 Aeroquip was acquired by Libby-Owens-Ford (LOF), the automotive and plate glass maker in Toledo, Ohio. My boss and I were transferred to the Toledo headquarters in 1972. My boss was made executive vice president of LOF and I continued to work on international affairs. I had a fancy title but little authority as LOF had little interest in foreign business.

One of my few projects with LOF was to help negotiate a joint venture with a Japanese company in Osaka. I had some experience with Japanese practices, having worked with a licensee and a joint venture partner in Japan. This new venture was the building of a plant on the Mexican border to make replacement windshields for

Japanese cars in the United States. It was to employ about a hundred people. We hired a young Mexican general manager who had already run such a plant in Mexico.

I went with our management team to Japan to finalize the agreement. We got safely through the negotiations, with the exception of the provision for supplying technical help to the proposed joint venture. We wanted to provide two men for a few months, but the Japanese group wanted many more people for an indefinite period. There was no way the venture could support such an expense and the Mexican manager didn't need that much help. After four days, we had exhausted all our explanations and were still deadlocked, and we only had one more day to complete the deal.

On the fourth evening while we were having cocktails, my counterpart on the Japanese negotiating team drew me aside. "Dick-san, why is your group so opposed to our technical assistance provision?" he asked.

I knew it was important for them to save face, but could see no way around the deadlock. "Because it is insane," I whispered.

"Ah, so," he whispered back. "That mean 'clazy.'"

"Yes," I replied.

"So," he ruminated, "clazy. Ah."

I thought I had probably sunk the venture, and the party broke up.

The next morning the head of the Japanese team greeted us. "Good morning," he said. "We agree with your position on the technical assistance provision."

Soon after, the Japanese group sent us a beautiful vase. Maybe my risky action had saved the venture after all.

■ ■ ■ ■ ■

My experiences with Caterpillar and Aeroquip convinced me to work only with the leader in any industry. When you are the leader you usually have the best products, the most capable people, and the best profits to maintain your position.

43

Twenty years working for those two companies provided me with invaluable business experience, which came in handy when Nancy and I opened a fly shop.

I DON'T FEEL COMFORTABLE HERE.

5 BIRTH OF THE KEEL FLY

Nancy got me my first fly rod when I started working for Aeroquip in 1963. In those days, you got rods at hardware or general sporting goods stores. Usually the employees were not fly fishers, and manufacturers had not yet started rating rods for line size (this practice didn't begin until 1965). What I got was a fiberglass rod that should have had a #8 line, but my line was a #5. If the fly line is too light or too heavy the rod may not cast well. My line was too light so it was tough to cast.

Although I already had a fly rod I visited fly shops wherever I traveled, trying to determine the best way to select a proper rod. But even the big-city stores in New York and London with fly-fishing departments were of little help when it came to selecting a rod. If you asked them to help you pick out a rod they would tell you they just loved this particular rod, or that one was Joe Brooks' favorite. So what?! I believed there should be a better way. Even then, I thought, "If ever I have a fly shop . . ."

The Fly Fishing Begins
The only fishing around Jackson, Michigan, was for bluegills and bass, so they were what I first fly fished for in small lakes. I was a tightwad

and did not want to spend money on a fishing boat, so I got my ten-year-old son, Sam, to accompany me on skin-diving trips to lakes to find a sunken rowboat to salvage. We found a small wooden boat in five feet of water and pulled it onto the bank with a rope. I was, of course, too cheap to paint it or to buy oars. Our lake was too deep to pole with a normal pole, but I solved that problem by getting a reinforcing rod, the kind used in concrete jobs. It was awkward but it worked.

Soon Sam became fed up with my penurious ways. One day he came home with a can of "Bimini blue" paint, a set of oars, and oarlocks that he bought. He fixed up the boat and christened it *Bimini Blue*. I was properly shamed and reimbursed him, which I expect he figured would happen all along.

※ ※ ※ ※ ※

I had read about trout fishing and decided to try it. I collected a bunch of fly-rod lures, mainly streamers but also some unweighted Colorado spinners and a tin imitation of a small minnow called a Tin Lizzie, after the Model T Ford. In my ignorance I assumed all fly-rod lures would qualify on "flies only" waters.

My first trout-fishing trip was to the Michigan Au Sable where I landed my first trout on the Tin Lizzie, which is a fly-rod lure, not a fly. I hooked the fish right on the boundary of the "flies only" water, which made it illegal. I'll never forget the thrill of landing my first trout on a fly rod, but I have to confess I started my trout-fishing career with an illegal lure.

The next season a friend of mine named Walt said I needed to learn to do it right. He invited me to spend some time fishing at his cabin on the Manistee River, where we went for opening day of trout. It was the time of the hendrickson hatch, of which I knew nothing at the time. I got up at dawn and fished until after dark that evening. Only later did I learn that the hendrickson is the main afternoon hatch early in the season, and the only productive time was late afternoon and early evening (or thereabouts) in the early spring. Still, I was thrilled. I caught three trout, but Walt caught five and his were bigger.

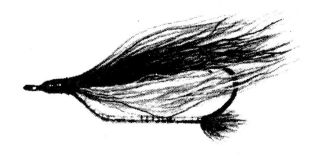

The Basic Keel Streamer

The hook shank acts as a keel and keeps the point upward riding over snags.

The Keel Fly

While fishing in the mid-1960s, I lost three streamers by snagging them on underwater logs. That pained me, having paid Orvis $1.75 each for those flies. It took me all weekend to figure out the solution. I altered my remaining streamers by twisting the dressing upside-down and bending the hook so the shank would act as a keel. The hook point would then ride upright, covered by the dressing, and the fly would slide right over the logs without snagging. It worked.

After some time, I decided the thing might be marketable, so I sought a name for it. My friend Stan Lievensee said it should be called the Keel Fly and the hook a Keel Hook. The name stuck.

Armed with an understanding of patents and licensing agree-ments, gained from my job at Aeroquip, I applied for patents and trademarks on the flies. The first patent search came up with a bunch of so-called "prior art" which meant that patents had been issued for lures that might be similar to mine. I had been aware such things existed but none of them worked. They simply buried the hook in a lot of hair, like a paintbrush, and would neither ride upright nor expose the hook if a fish struck.

My patent attorney was not able to convince the examiner of the validity of our claims, so I duplicated all the conflicting designs and went to the patent office in Washington, D.C., with a water pan to demonstrate the difference. The examiner was unimpressed. He said it did not matter if the competing devices didn't work—the written claims were the important thing, and they claimed to work. I asked him, if I presented claims for an airplane that would not fly, would it be patentable? He said yes, provided the claims had not been previ-ously allowed in a patent.

I was stymied, but my attorney said he would resubmit the claims and we would get a different examiner. He did and we got a different examiner who granted our claims.

I had been aware that Herter's, a mail-order company specializ-ing in hunting and fishing gear, offered several lures that were copies of other makers' lures, but with a different trademark. Johnson's Silver

Minnow was offered in Herter's catalog as Jensen's Silver Minnow, and the famous Dardevle was listed as the Devilfish. An imitation of the Keel Fly appeared as the Rudder Fly, and the Keel Hook was the Rudder Hook. My lawyer investigated and found out that the district court for Waseca, Minnesota, where Herter's was located, had a reputation of practically never upholding a U.S. patent or trademark. The whole thing was not worth the expense of filing a lawsuit so I just had to let it ride.

I took lessons in fly tying and tried to find experienced tiers who could produce my Keel Flies. I knew what the flies should look like but could not produce good examples. As I worked on designing flies and finding fly tiers, I found help from a friend, Bing McClellan. Bing and I both worked at Aeroquip and lived a couple of doors apart. His son Bingo and my son Sam were best friends. The four of us fished together, and the boys built forts in the woods between our homes. This was around 1966, and by then I knew a little bit about fishing streamers and dry flies.

Bing left Aeroquip and bought a company called Burke Products that specialized in making fishing lures. "Put a Burke where they lurk" was their slogan. Since he already had the sales force he was pleased to acquire a license to make and sell the Keel Flies. He created the Keel Fly Co. to conduct the fly business.

A. J. McClane was fishing editor of *Field & Stream* magazine as well as author of the *Standard Fishing Encyclopedia* and several other books. Bing had long been friends with A. J. and told him about the Keel Flies. In 1969 A. J. headlined them in *Field & Stream*: "The Keel Hook—Revolution in Fly Fishing." His article ran several pages and showed pictures of the flies and explained how they worked.

By 1970 Bing had the Keel Flies in stores around the country. His company made streamer flies, wet flies, dry flies, bass bugs, and saltwater flies, in a variety of patterns. A. J. McClane named the bass bug Bing had designed on a Keel Hook the "Miracle Bug." Guy de la Valdene, who was well known in saltwater fly-rodding circles, caught a world record thirty-pound permit on the Keel pink shrimp saltwater pattern.

The Keel Flies were carried by Orvis, Abercrombie & Fitch, and other major retailers. They were written about by famous writers like Lefty Kreh, Dave Whitlock, Nelson Bryant of the *New York Times*, and Tom McNally of the *Chicago Tribune*. They were then picked up by Abu-Garcia, the well-regarded Swedish tackle maker, and Dermot Wilson, the British fly-fishing expert who operated a catalog fly-fishing company. Dermot was especially drawn to the dry flies with the curved body of a mayfly. He stated in his catalog that they cocked and floated and hooked better than conventional flies.

In the early 1970s I negotiated a buyback of the Keel Fly Co. My wife Nancy operated the company while I continued working in international business for Aeroquip. I also wrote articles for *Fly Fisherman Magazine* and *Fly Rod & Reel*. This all led to my starting work on a book, for which Bing had suggested the title *Fish the Impossible Places*. The story behind that book, which took several years to write and publish, is told in the chapter "The $2.50 Manuscript."

No One Is Going to Leave . . .
You might think it would be obvious that purchasing decisions in a fly-fishing company would be handled or approved by anglers but this is not always so. One time I walked into Abercrombie's in New York. They were once a leader in the outdoors business but were switching over to clothing. I was looking for a weight-forward #6 floating line—probably the most important line in fly fishing—but the clerk said they did not have any. I asked if he could get me one. He replied he was not allowed to. I said the Scientific Anglers rep could get it. He said he was not allowed to talk to reps. I asked who made these decisions. He said the treasurer. Good grief!

This was during the period when Abercrombie & Fitch was going through several different owners. The new owners had no knowledge of fly fishing. Nevertheless, they had ordered some Keel Flies from us, but had not paid for them for several months, after many promises. Since I was in town, I decided to pay the company's treasurer a visit. He was polite and promised to pay soon. I told him I could guarantee that. When he asked why I said it that way, I replied that I had nowhere I needed to go, and no one was going to leave his office until I had the check, even if it took all night. I had the check in jig time.

THE SISTERS DON'T FOOL AROUND.

DON'T PROSCUATE ME, BRO!

John Voelker told me Charles Kuralt had found this sign. Charles was a favorite friend of John's, and Charles described John as the closest thing to a great man he had ever known.

I did not want to be proscuated as a vialtor, so I quit congretating.

6 JOHN VOELKER & *TROUT MADNESS*

To help perfect the Keel Flies, I gave samples to my fly-fishing co-workers at Aeroquip, who tried them out and gave me advice. I also started to contact famous anglers. One of the first was John Voelker, a well-known Michigan writer. John had written several books under the pseudonym Robert Traver.

My introduction to angling literature was through John's book *Trout Madness*. It intrigued me as a beginning fly fisherman, with such humor as "Fly fishing is so much fun, it should be done in bed," or his idea that fly fishing was "high seduction as compared to rape." For many years, I reread that book every winter to remind myself of the pleasures of the trout season.

Michigan has produced a number of major fly-fishing authors. Arnold Gingrich, originally from Michigan, was founder and editor of *Esquire* magazine and the author of the fly-fishing books *The Well Tempered Angler*, *The Joys of Trout*, and *The Fishing in Print* before World War II. Postwar, Nick Lyons and Ernie Schwiebert did some of their early fishing and writing in Michigan during their college days. John Voelker, who hailed from the small town of Ishpeming in the Upper Peninsula, was one of the favorites in the 1950s. Carl Richards and Doug Swisher were the most prominent of the newer writers starting in 1970.

I sent John some Keel Flies and asked him what he thought of them. He wrote back and said he thought the idea was great and suggested that I personally bring him some more that we could fish with. He said to arrive at night. He fished all day, every day, during the trout season, so I could only call him at night to tell him I had arrived.

John picked me up the morning after my arrival at the hotel, the charming, if slightly worn, Mather Inn. My first impression was that of a totally genial man. As time went by, I learned he was more than that. He was a prince. John was always nice to everybody, especially fishermen. If you fished you were invited to fish with him. He was also an excellent correspondent. He answered every letter almost immediately using a green felt-tipped pen.

John, then in his sixties, looked like John Wayne and talked with Wayne's gravelly voice. He could be a bit crusty, but he was never malicious. To know John you also had to know one or another incarnation of his "fish car," named Buckshot. A fish car is a vehicle largely devoted to supporting its owner on fishing trips. Buckshot is described in *Trout Madness*, where John goes on for several pages listing all the equipment he had stashed inside. There were five rods slung from the car ceiling, binoculars, a camera, a magnifying glass, four sizes of flashlights, a lantern, waders, hip boots, low boat boots, detailed maps of Michigan, a bedroll, blankets, a tarpaulin, a pup tent, a Primus stove and cook kit, canteens, and a small portable icebox. And then there was patching cement, ferrule cement, rain clothes and a change of street clothes, two axes, one brush knife, pruning shears, a leather punch, a hammer and nails, a pry bar, and a .38 revolver. Left out of his description was all the usual fishing gear that would take a page itself.

There was always a boat on top of Buckshot, and nautical gear inside. John did, however, leave the front seat clear. "Indeed," he said, "sometimes I have even managed to squeeze an adventurous small fisherman in the back seat." This was no exaggeration. My son Sam went along once and it took John a half hour to free up enough space in the back to squeeze him in.

John and I spent a few days fishing and critiquing the Keel Flies. He gave me several ideas on how and where to sell them and suggested I promote them by writing a book on fishing and tying the flies.

John was an old-style angler, and I attribute that to the fact that many Upper Peninsula streams are not major hatch rivers. I now know that in streams with few hatches almost any fly will take a fish or two now and then. John fished only with split cane rods, and he preferred the slower ones as he mainly roll-cast on his beloved beaver dam ponds. His favorite fly when I knew him was the jassid, which does not imitate anything I know of in Michigan, though it is said to imitate some type of small beetle. He loved and wrote about old-fashioned flies such as the McGinty. It imitated a bee, which is not a major trout food. He also wrote of the Betty McNault, which I had never heard of before or since.

Fishing with John

John loved his little beaver dam pond, which he called Uncle Tom's Pond when he talked to his friends, and Frenchman's Pond in his books. He always caught a few eight-inch brook trout, which are common in the Upper Peninsula.

Once on the way to the pond, John and I stopped at a convenience store. I decided to get a six-pack of beer and put it on the counter. The clerk said she could not sell beer before noon on Sunday. Then she looked over at John and said, "John, you old son of a bitch, why didn't you tell me he was with you?" She sold me the beer, Sunday notwithstanding, while John stood chuckling.

I fished with John once each summer for many years. After a combined career as a lawyer, prosecutor, Michigan Supreme Court judge, and writer, he retired to the Upper Peninsula. After he retired from the Supreme Court, I told him that a lawyer friend had said John wrote the best briefs of court cases, and each month he waited eagerly to read them. John chuckled and said, "Some people say I wrote my best fiction in those briefs." Fishing with John was enjoyed more for conversation with an amazing man than for the fishing itself.

JOHN VOELKER AT HIS BEAVER DAM POND.

"It's not a sport. It's a vice."

Anatomy of a Murder

John's magnum opus, *Anatomy of a Murder*, is a masterpiece of suspense. Some say it was the predecessor of courtroom dramas such as those by John Grisham. The book was number one for twenty-nine weeks on the *New York Times* best-seller list. The movie version was directed by Otto Preminger and starred Jimmy Stewart, George C. Scott, and Lee Remick, major movie stars in the 1950s. Duke Ellington composed the music for the movie, and they all came together with John in Ishpeming and Marquette, Michigan, where the movie was filmed in 1959. When filming ended, they gathered with John in Gigs Gagliardi's Roosevelt Bar in Ishpeming, where Ellington played the piano for the festivities. (Gigs was John's closest friend, known to all John's devotees.)

* * * * *

On a visit in 1969, as we headed to John's fishing cabin, he said, "I should have told you I can't fish late tonight. All my daughters and their husbands and kids are here. This is my sixty-fifth birthday, and they're having a dinner for me this evening." After fishing that afternoon we headed toward John's car, where he pulled out a bottle of Bourbon and handed me an old tin cup. I protested that I didn't drink whiskey, to which he replied: "Listen, goddamit, this is my sixty-fifth birthday, and you are going to drink a proper toast. Besides, if it's good enough for Lee Remick, it's good enough for you!" The Bourbon tasted better after that sales pitch, but I'm sure John got a bigger kick out of serving Lee Remick than serving me.

The John Voelker Foundation

When John was in his seventies, two of his fans, Rich Vander Veen and Fred Baker Jr., came up with the idea of a John Voelker Foundation. When they approached John about it, he agreed but said having a foundation named for him made him feel "a wee bit embalmed." Actually, John often joked about "feeling embalmed" after a few drinks—he did love his Bourbon.

The John Voelker Foundation, working with *Fly Rod & Reel*

magazine, sponsors an annual writing contest for the best original article or essay promoting fly fishing or related conservation. Charles Kuralt called this the most prestigious outdoors fiction prize in America. It has resulted in as many as one hundred submissions a year, eighteen of which were recently published by Fly Rod & Reel Books in a volume titled *In Hemingway's Meadow*. Nick Lyons edited and published a posthumous book, *Traver on Fishing*, which included some of Voelker's earlier works, under the auspices of the foundation.

John felt strongly that American Indians were often discriminated against, a theme he addressed in *Laughing Whitefish*, a story about an Indian woman who spent much of her life seeking justice for her father, who had been cheated of his legal rights in the UP. John fostered a scholarship that is awarded annually to a Native American seeking a legal education. So far this scholarship has resulted in about twenty students gaining their law degrees.

We'll Go Partners

John would often send me a message out of the blue so I wasn't surprised when I received the following:

> Dear Dick,
> I have a great idea! And we'll go partners. We will take night crawlers, toughen them up so they will stay on a hook, and bottle them and sell them. We'll make a mint! Let me know what you think.
> Warm regards.
> John

I thought he was joking, and wrote back, "I think people would drum us both out of the fly fishing corps if we started selling worms." I thought it was a catchy response. I did not tell him that bottled night crawlers had been sold in bait and tackle stores for a long time as I assumed he knew that.

The response was catchy all right. I caught hell. John wrote back that I had no appreciation for a good idea and that was the last time he would waste one on me. Fortunately, John was too good-natured to hold a grudge, so after a short hiatus I was once more welcome in the Upper Peninsula.

The Upper Peninsula and Its Yoopers

To understand John Voelker and the Upper Peninsula (or "UP") of Michigan, you have to know about the "yoopers," as the residents of the UP are called. It is always fun to be among the yoopers, who are predominantly descendants of the immigrants who came to the area to work in the logging camps or mines. Finns, Swedes, and Italians were among the most numerous, with a sprinkling from the rest of Europe. Some supplemented their income by poaching or bootlegging.

John had a strong affection for the area and the people, and his novels were mainly about the yoopers. He was not happy about the encroachment of civilization. He resisted the plan to build a bridge from the Lower Peninsula to the Upper, and claimed he was chair of the "Bomb the Bridge Committee." John was certainly right that the bridge would cause migration from the south, but the yoopers live on undiluted. The bridge is, in fact, an impressive piece of engineering. It is one of the world's longest suspension bridges, extending five miles from shoreline to shoreline. Yoopers refer to residents of the Lower Peninsula as "trolls" because they live below the bridge.

I can drive for many miles in the UP without seeing any funny signs, or anything except evergreen trees for that matter. The trees have to eke a living out of the two inches of topsoil that have formed on top of the granite that the glaciers had scraped bare. Glaciers scraped away much of the limestone, which is the primary natural enrichment for most good trout streams, and dumped it in our rich Lower Peninsula streams. Lower Michigan consists of glacial deposits that were dumped into a huge limestone bowl that once was the bottom of an ancient sea.

The Blast

Backwoods humor in Michigan's Upper Peninsula tends to be farther out than in many other far-out places. To while away the miles while traveling in the UP, I would listen to a disk jockey on the car radio who told stories between tunes.

One story concerned a sportsman who had recently died. He loved to shoot skeet at his local gun club. In his will he expressed his wish to be cremated with his ashes packed into shotgun shells that his loyal gun club brothers were to fire off at their spring outing, followed by a few drinks in his memory. The report is they had a blast! I suspect they also got blasted.

Pure Yooper

John Giuliani is a well-known guide from the Canadian side of the St. Mary's River. He invited John Voelker and me to fish for Atlantic salmon in the St. Marys at Sault Sainte Marie, but John was not able to go. Our party required two cars, and I was assigned to the car driven by Giuliani's father, Alberto. I was delighted. Alberto told me stories of his immigration to Canada from Italy after WWII. He was willing to trust North America with his life, but he brought his own garlic plants, which he was still cultivating forty years later.

Alberto was renowned as a fisherman who caught and ate a lot of fish. However, he assured me in his husky voice, "Gianni, he's-a educating me. He's-a teaching me all about that Orvis stuff, and catch-and-release, and all that. I don't kill many salmon any more. This year, I only kept sixty-five Atlantics, enough to make spaghetti sauce." I was glad there were no catch-and-release purists in the car.

■ ■ ■ ■ ■

I arranged for John to come to Grand Rapids to address our local Trout Unlimited chapter in the late 1980s. After his speech, one of our members asked him to what they owed the honor of his presence. John thought for a minute, then said, "I did it for Dick and I'll be damned if I'll ever do it again."

A TOUCH-UP, PLEASE. THE WORD IS *PARTS*.

7 THE 2^{50} MANUSCRIPT

Around 1968, Bing McClellan of Burke Products and John Voelker encouraged me to write a book on Keel Flies, including how to tie and fish them. In my ignorance, I figured all you needed to write a book was to start writing. It honestly never occurred to me that I could not simply sit at a typewriter and tell the story. It took many evenings on a Royal portable over a couple of years to complete the manuscript. I would not try that again without a computer! It was a hell of a job, with each correction requiring retyping every page after the correction using carbon paper and onionskin to provide copies.

When the manuscript was complete I took Bing's suggestion and titled it *Fish the Impossible Places.* I asked John Voelker who I should approach to publish it, and he suggested Nick Lyons from New York City. Nick had published dozens of fly-fishing books, and was preeminent in that field. He steered me to Freshet Press.

Freshet Press was a small publisher of fly-fishing books that used employees of major New York publishers who moonlighted at home to edit, design, and print their books. They were in the process of publishing a book by Poul Jorgenson and another by Charlie Fox, both well-known authors. The owners of Freshet, Bud Frasca and Mike Cohen, said they wanted to publish my book, and reserved the

WHAT KIND OF BAR IS THAT?

right to make changes. I agreed to that provided they would first let me take a crack at any necessary improvements, to which they agreed.

Bud and Mike then introduced me to my editor. After he had reviewed the manuscript, we got together for dinner. He could not have been nicer. He told me my book was wonderful, which should have been the tip-off, and that it was so well written all he had to do was check it for minor errors such as punctuation. He could do it in a couple of weeks. From that point on it was nothing but promises and excuses. I kept after him, and Bud Frasca even had his son, Buddy, stake out his apartment in Gramercy Park on weekends, but none of us could ever catch him.

A year later, Bud spotted my editor on the street and called him over.

"What has happened to our manuscript?" Bud asked.

"Do you have $2.50?" the editor replied.

"Sure. Why?"

"I hocked Dick's manuscript in this bar over here, and for $2.50 I can get it for you."

With the edited manuscript finally in hand it was time to turn it over to a book designer. Book designers do a lot of technical work. They choose the page size, paper, type style, and so on. Freshet hired a young employee from one of the big New York publishers to do the design. She kept promising to finish the job in a couple of weeks then gave excuses and made more promises. Finally I went to her office and asked to see what she had done. I had provided over a hundred photographs of fishing and fly tying. Each picture had been placed in a duly labeled envelope that included a positive print, a negative, and a slip with the caption. The designer had emptied the contents of all the envelopes into a box and had no idea how to sort them out.

We were lucky that Joan Stoliar was willing to straighten out the mess. Joan was a respected book designer (she had designed *Jonathan Livingston Seagull*), and she was a friend of Bud's. She effectively did the design on the book, which was finally published in 1974. Lefty Kreh wrote a generous introduction to the book after testing the bass and saltwater versions of the Keel Fly.

But that was not the end of the story. The publisher printed ten thousand copies of the book, but only bound five thousand, postponing the binding of the rest until later. The five thousand bound copies of the book were sold, but slowly, as the market for fly-fishing books had gone soft. Bud decided he could not sell the remaining five thousand and scrapped the pages, along with the printing plates, so that was that. It had gone to the "impossible places." The market revived, but too late. Fortunately I was not dependent on this project for a living.

DERMOT WILSON FISHING ON THE RIVER ITCHEN.

"Could you bring one of those new graphite rods so we can fish it this weekend?"—Dermot Wilson

8 DERMOT WILSON'S ENGLAND

Much of my overseas travel for Aeroquip was in Great Britain as the company had licensees in England and Scotland. None of my business contacts wanted to spend their weekends entertaining me so I took the opportunity to explore British fishing.

In 1970 I got a letter from Dermot Wilson, asking how he could get Keel Hooks. I ended up granting him a license to make the flies in Great Britain. He was the first to see the advantage of using the hooks for dry flies as they were curved like the body of a mayfly. Dermot claimed in his fly-fishing catalog that these flies cocked and floated better than traditional flies.

Dermot Wilson was the author of the English best seller *Fishing the Dry Fly*, and was the fly-fishing guru of England. He had resigned from the British Army (to which his family had generations of service) as a major with two decorations after World War II, around age twenty. One of the decorations was the Military Cross, which he was awarded for leading a patrol behind enemy lines. Always modest, Dermot later claimed, "I didn't deserve it, I just got lost."

After the war, Dermot joined the J. Walter Thompson advertising agency in London. I have been told that he was the most highly acclaimed copy writer in London. Named the youngest director of J.

Walter Thompson at the age of thirty-seven, Dermot chose to leave all that behind and start a fly-fishing service. He bought The Mill at Nether Wallop near Stockbridge in Hampshire, where he lived and maintained a fly shop. He published a fly-fishing catalog and provided fine chalk stream fishing on the famous rivers Test and Itchen, England's premier chalk streams.

Dermot owned fishing rights on five beats on the Test and Itchen. (A beat is a stretch of river where fishing is permitted.) By virtue of our business relationship, I had free run of his beats whenever I was in England. By that time, I had learned the basics of fishing a dry fly. After several trips to the Test and Itchen, I was a moderately competent angler. Those beats were later acquired by Orvis, and they still offer fishing there.

Fishing the English Chalk Streams

I learned about British fishing rules on my first visit to the Itchen. The thing to remember is that the rules are determined by the beat owner, so you have to ask what the rules are. Dermot sent me out with his bailiff, and I asked him about the rules. "You can keep one fish over eighteen inches, and two small fish for breakfast," the bailiff explained.

English chalk streams are very rich and produce an abundance of insects and fish. The fish are fussy, but they tend to feed most of the time, and you get plenty of chances to present a fly to rising fish. They tend to be large because the proprietors make sure not many are killed. The closest thing to this kind of fishing that I have experienced in America is on the spring creeks of the Yellowstone Valley and some of the eastern spring creeks.

During my early fishing years I probably fished as much, or more, in England as in the United States. British knowledge of aquatic entomology was every bit as good as that in the States; however, at that time, the British had not been as creative as American anglers in developing artificial fly patterns to imitate natural flies.

Dermot showed me many of the techniques used by English chalk stream anglers. On chalk streams it is common to approach fish from downstream, as the fish's vision is focused upstream. After spotting a good feeding fish, I was advised to retreat downstream and hook and release all the smaller fish down the river so they would not spook the prime target. Next I was to mark the location of the target fish and back off until I could not see it. Presumably if I could not see the fish with my Polaroids, the fish could not see me.

I would then cast above the location of the fish. Dermot told me that the fish would often take the fly without my being aware of it. In this clear water, I should not wait to see the fish rise, but watch for the flash of the fish's white sides and belly turning under the fly, then set the hook in anticipation of the take. It is a tactic I have since found useful when trout are being highly selective in clear water. I later learned to strike when the fly approached the spot where the fish had last been seen rising, a technique that works well when it starts to get dark.

Rods and Attire

In the early 1970s, Dermot asked me to bring him one of the brand-new graphite rods, as graphite rods were not then being made in the British Isles. I scrambled and got one delivered to the departure lounge at Idlewild (now Kennedy) Airport minutes before boarding.

Dermot arranged for the two of us and two British friends to take turns using the graphite rod and to say nothing about it until the end of the day. I expected my hosts to be very conservative, and felt ill at ease when Dermot said I should be the first to report, since I had brought the rod. I said I did not feel experienced enough to judge fly rods, but that it was by far the best rod I had ever fished. The other three instantly responded: "I agree." "I agree." "I agree." It was a revelation for all of us.

Dermot contributed to my knowledge of rods in many ways. After checking out a couple of cane rods in his shop labeled "Wallop Brook," I told him I wanted to buy one, and asked him which one I should choose. He told me to take both out and try them, and to decide for myself. He said there was no way anyone could tell what rod another person would like. It turned out that I loved one, but not the other. Once again, I mused over the idea that someday I might have a fly shop, and I knew I would want clients to try out the rods before purchasing them.

There is a difference not only in the type of fishing attire worn in England, but also in the reasons why certain items are worn. Hip boots in England are of the usual variety, but they are not intended primarily for wading in the streams. Instead, they are worn mainly for kneeling on the wet bank, to avoid being silhouetted against the sky, and to hide behind shrubbery, thus hidden from the fish.

Vests are a whole other matter. One day after we had fished together a few times, Dermot said, "I think it's bloody silly that we still fish in coats and ties, and I've been eyeing your vest. Would you be so kind as to bring me one of those vests next trip?" Of course I said I would, and I did. Even though Lee Wulff had shown Dermot his vest some years earlier, vests had not caught on in England. Dermot did wear the vest I brought him when he fished with me but I never saw another British angler pictured with a vest afterward.

I Am Sweet Thing . . .

Since I was traveling on business, I could not manage bulky tackle, so I got light, compact equipment. I ordered a telescopic fly rod from Japan, which was only inches long when collapsed. The directions were amusing: "I am sweet thing. Take me out and shake me." The rod was made of about eight pieces, so it was powerful, but I would only have chosen it when I had to. I don't even remember when I disposed of the rod.

The Mill at Nether Wallop

Dermot's shop and home were in an old mill at Nether Wallop. (Ed Zern, the famous fishing humorist, said Nether Wallop was English for "low blow.") The mill wheel had been disconnected, but the water still ran through the millhouse. Dermot had installed a glass wall in one of the millraces so people could watch trout feed. I called it a "fluvarium" (a flowing water aquarium). The trout were confined in the fluvarium by grills at either end. The mill stream brought them all the food they needed year-round and we could watch how the fish looked at and took the insects that came their way.

At Winchester Cathedral, a few miles from Dermot's shop, you can see the grave of the famous fishing writer Izaak Walton in the cathedral's floor. What would ordinarily be a headstone becomes, I suppose, a bodystone when laid flat in the floor. I came across it when the sun was shining through the stained glass windows. I'm not very emotional or religious, but it felt holy to me anyway, and I stopped at a local pub and hoisted a half-pint in the old gent's honor.

A Moderately Fine Grayling Stream

In anticipation of a weekend's fishing out of his home at Nether Wallop, Dermot told me to meet him at the London Angler's Club on Friday evening, to ride to Hampshire with him after he addressed the club. After the speech a member asked him, "Tell me, Dermot, what is your view of the relative merits of the Test and the Itchen?" (This was a widely debated subject in England at the time. I haven't been back for decades, but I imagine it is still in controversy. When you own local fishing rights, you stick to your stream.)

Dermot replied, "Well, the Test is a moderately fine grayling stream." This set off a chorus of cheers and jeers, because that is like saying the Beaverkill is good for carp. Fortunately, Dermot was a widely respected and beloved member of the angling fraternity, so he could pull comments like that off. He was one of the friendliest and most pleasant people I have ever met—one of those rare souls who naturally get along with almost everyone. Dermot could have any angling group gathered about him in short order, taking in every word he spoke.

Coarse Fishermen

Dermot's bailiff explained to me that he allowed "coarse fishermen" to fish his river beats with the proviso they would only kill coarse fish, except they could keep a trout or two as compensation for getting rid of the roach, tench, dace, and grayling. There was nothing coarse about the skills these fishermen possessed, nor was there anything coarse about their character. They rivaled any fly angler in skill. It was interesting to watch them with their delicate and sensitive fishing methods. They used long, light spinning rods with one- or two-pound-test line and the quill from a feather for a float, which dipped whenever a fish touched their bait.

The World's Worst Ghillie

Dermot told me the story of an American angler fishing for salmon in Scotland with a Scottish ghillie, or guide. He did not get a strike all day. At the end of the day, the exasperated American said, "Do you suppose it is possible that in the entire world I happened to draw the worst ghillie?" The ghillie instantly responded, "Oh no, sir! That would be entirely too great a coincidence!" The coincidence would be that the world's worst ghillie should happen to encounter the world's worst angler.

EVERY BAR SHOULD GIVE SUCH SERVICE.

9 LONDON & BEYOND

In the early 1970s it was hard to get a room in London during the summer. I was fortunate, however, to get acquainted with Monsieur Gustave, the elegant, formally attired Swiss manager of the splendid Connaught Hotel. I frequently had to go to London on short notice, but M. Gustave told me I could just come in without a reservation and he would probably be able to find me a room. The hotel reserved a few smaller rooms for such needs. Once it was a cot in a meeting room, but there was always a room.

I think M. Gustave was surprised that I was so relaxed about arriving at the hotel without a reservation. He simply enjoyed the challenge of putting me up. I never told him that three of my best friends—a PhD candidate at the London School of Economics, a broker at a Merrill Lynch office, and a managing director of an investment bank—had homes in London, and I could have stayed with them if I needed digs.

The investment banker, Joe Baird, whom I had known in Panama, was credited with creating the Eurodollar market when he was only in his forties. He was a fly fisherman, so I invited him to come with me to Dermot Wilson's place to fish one weekend. He accepted the invitation, and offered to drive. You can imagine my surprise when he showed up in a chauffeur-driven Rolls Royce. I was flabbergasted, but felt like royalty while we toured in luxury through the Hampshire hills.

During the weekend Joe commented that he admired the fact that I would always take time to fish whereas he was always too busy. I replied that this probably explained why he was in his position and I was in mine. He went on to become president of Occidental Petroleum. I became a clerk in a fly shop.

Another of our investment bankers invited me to dinner at Claridges Hotel. When we arrived for dinner and were seated, the sommelier showed the banker a wine list. The banker glanced at it and said he wanted the private wine list, and the sommelier brought another. They carried on a lengthy discussion about the wines, and when they were finished I asked the banker how he knew so much about wine. He replied, "My mother is the wife of the owner of the Château Lafitte-Rothschild." (The Château Lafitte-Rothschild is one of France's premier wineries.)

Dinner with Max

One of my English business contacts, Barry Heath, specialized in fishing for sharks in the English Channel, and when he learned I was a fellow fisherman he was eager to talk. I told him about downriggers, and he invited me to fish for sharks with him on the next trip. Downriggers are used for trolling in deep water. A heavy weight is let down on a line that is attached by a trigger mechanism to a lure on another line. When a fish takes the lure the lure is released and the fish can be fought on an unweighted line.

On the next trip, my wife, Nancy, accompanied me. I brought Barry some downrigger gear and off we went into the English Channel in Barry's forty-foot boat. We immediately found the rough seas for which the channel is notorious. The bow of the boat would ride high on the peak of a wave and then smack down hard into the trough, and the foredeck would be covered by the next wave. The wind was strong enough to blow a hatch cover off. Barry's crewman, who was probably in his sixties, turned various shades of pale, which did not reassure us. I was concerned with staying afloat but Nancy was worried that the steak and kidney pie that had been brought on board and left unrefrigerated would do us in.

The channel was too rough to fish so we headed ashore to Barry's town house on the Isle of Wight, where we were spending the weekend. Barry and his wife advised us we would be having dinner at their friend Max's house that evening but were evasive when we sought more information about Max.

At dinnertime the four of us went downstairs to the nautical equivalent of an unpainted tack room. We were invited to duck our heads and walk through a low door. Barry's lower level opened into the upper level of a town house that was one street down. That house belonged to Max. Inside was a posh nautical museum with a long dinner table set for a hundred guests. Among the many exhibits was a huge oil painting of Lord Nelson's flagship at Trafalgar, the HMS *Victory*. The museum also contained the actual helm of the *Victory*.

Liveried waiters served us a sumptuous meal. During dinner I turned to Barry and said, "OK, now tell me the real story. Who is Max?" Barry explained that he and our host, Max Aitken, were in the RAF during World War II and flew Spitfires, along with Group Captain Peter Townsend, consort of Princess Margaret. Max was the son of Lord Beaverbrook and owned many pharmacies, the employees of which were among our fellow dinner guests. Fishing invitations can lead you into remarkable situations.

Packington Estate

My work on the acquisition of an English factory required me to make numerous trips to the Midlands industrial area. I had been invited to fish the River Blythe on Packington Estate, which belonged to the Earl of Aylesford, by the earl's bailiff, or overseer, Tony. Tony introduced me to the earl, a genial man who wished me good fishing.

On my first visit to Packington Estate, I inscribed in their logbook that the visit had given me the chance to test my Keel Fly on

English water. The bailiff was enthusiastic. He said, "Oh, jolly good. Usually they write 'bloody awful fishing' or some such." There were no fish rising that day so I was reduced to wet flies, but several trout were taken, and the chef at my hotel prepared them for me chilled.

When I arrived at the estate on another occasion, Tony was not in but had left instructions with two of his children that I was there to fish. They cheerfully showed me the way, accompanied by another boy, who was just a little older. After a while I asked the older boy if he too was one of Tony's children. He replied in a low tone that would ice a penguin, "You are joking," and stalked off, leaving Tony's kids to explain that he was heir to the title and estate. I guessed that when he became the Earl of Aylesford my fishing rights would be terminated.

■ ■ ■ ■ ■

Returning from Packington to the Connaught Hotel in London one rainy Sunday evening, I discovered a diplomatic reception was in full swing in the lobby. Everyone was in formal dress and many were wearing sashes and medals of all sorts. I had been fishing and was wearing wet blue jeans and a rain jacket.

M. Gustave quickly headed me off at the door with a "Good evening, Mr. Pobst."

"Good evening, M'sieu Gustave," I replied. "I've just come in from the country."

He smiled and said, "I know, sir." He then hustled me down a side hall and into the elevator.

Izaak Walton Country

Trout country is always beautiful, but none of it is better than the English countryside. I loved the mornings and evenings driving through the Cotswolds and the Derbyshire hills when I knew a stream waited for me at the end of the journey.

You can fish the River Dove in Derbyshire—the home water of Izaak Walton, author of *The Compleat Angler*. If you stay at the Izaak Walton Hotel in Dovedale, near Ashbourn you are entitled to fish their private water. I caught a couple of trout from the Dove. The chef prepared them for me poached, chilled, and wonderful. I liked the atmosphere of the old hotel, and the dining room was excellent.

Trooping of the Colors

When my Merrill Lynch friend found out that I had an upcoming Saturday free he offered me tickets to a ceremony called the Trooping of the Colors. Clueless, I asked him what it was, and he explained that it is a parade in honor of the Queen's birthday, in which stately, polished, mounted regiments paraded with the royal carriage.

The day of the event, Nancy and I headed to the Horse Guard Parade Ground and found our seats. Next to us sat an attractive couple who were much more elegantly dressed than we were. The young man was dressed in a gray formal cutaway and trousers, a vest, a ruffled shirt, and a tall gray top hat. Whenever we had questions about the ceremony the man would turn and answer them. He knew everything. I asked him how he came to know so much about the proceedings, and he replied in a deep, elegant tone, "I *commawnd* the Royal Horse Guard." That worked.

IS THIS A LISTING, OR THEIR HQ?

10 UNDERSTANDING THE BRITISH

Even when you are in an English-speaking country there is no guarantee the people will understand your English, or vice versa. You may need to know Cockney, Geordie, and even Robert Burns as well.

The Geordies

One day I was headed north, bound for Alnwick (pronounced *ah-nick*), home of Hardy Bros., the leading British tackle maker, for a meeting with its president. Jim Hardy and I got acquainted over a nice lunch, but Jim was not free to fish that weekend. He did, however, steer me to the Tillmouth Park Hotel on the River Till, a tributary of Scotland's River Tweed just south of the Scottish border.

Upon my arrival at the hotel, I went straight to the pub to see if there were any fishermen there so I could pick their brains. I sat down and greeted the man on my right. His first words were, "Wr jrdys, yno."

He kept repeating the phrase so I turned to the man on my left and asked him for enlightenment. He said the first man had said, "We're Geordies, you know."

I asked him what that meant and he explained, "It means they speak a dialect of English you'll never understand, much more difficult than Cockney."

I have never understood a word of Cockney, which they say is spoken by anyone born within the sound of the church bells of St. Mary-Le-Bow. "Do you fish?" I asked my pub mate on the left. He said he did not, so I decided to take my chances and just fish the river. It was beautiful hill country, and I fished a stretch of the river that was crossed by a Roman aqueduct that had a swan beneath it, guarding its nest. I only caught one fish, but it was a twenty-inch brown and it made my evening.

The Land of Robert Burns

The next morning I crossed over the ruins of Hadrian's Wall (which was built by the Roman legions to keep the barbarians out) into Scotland to spend my Sunday sightseeing. There I chanced on a field trial of sheep dogs, mainly border collies. I will never cease to be amazed at the skill the shepherds and their dogs exhibit when they divide up the sheep and herd them into groups. The dogs follow the orders of the shepherds who use both spoken commands and hand signals, often from way across a field.

I spied a half-dozen tweed-wearing, distinguished-looking Scottish gentlemen standing in a circle, apparently enjoying their day in the sun, and thought I'd edge over and see what they were doing. It turned out that each of them had a glass tumbler in his hand, and one of them had a bottle, obviously Scotch whisky. The man with the bottle poured each man a glass, then lifted his glass and said, "Let's get dronk!"

The following day I had a meeting in Glasgow. My contact there asked, "Have you ever been to a buns dinna?" It took a while, but I finally realized he was saying, "Have you ever been to a Burns dinner?" The Burns dinner is an annual celebration of Robert Burns' birthday. The men go and recite Burns' poetry, little of which I could understand, except for the line from his poem "To a Louse":

O wad some Pow'r the giftie gie us
To see oursels as others see us!

Everybody knows this quote, but few realize Burns was watching a louse crawl on the bonnet of an otherwise attractive young woman.

At the Burns dinner, whisky is drunk in ample quantities, which I could never do, and they eat haggis, which is a pudding composed of odd innards of sheep and oatmeal cooked in the sheep's stomach, which I happen to like. It might put you off if I described it further, but to me it is ambrosia.

＊ ＊ ＊ ＊ ＊

Following the Burns dinner I took a train back to the Midlands. We were slowing down for a station, so I asked a young woman sharing my compartment, "Do you know what town we are coming to?" As if she had been mortally insulted, she turned her back to me and stared out the window. Suddenly she turned back and said, "Screw!" I was really embarrassed. What should I say? Thank you? Then I saw the sign at the station, and realized she had said "It's Crewe."

The Mods

You may recall the days when many young people in England followed the style of either the mods or the rockers. The mods dressed very neatly but the rockers were hippies. These changing patterns of dress and behavior among youngsters were hard for many traditional Britishers to stomach.

Farther down the train line, while I was having a cup of coffee in the lunch car, a florid, weighty Colonel Blimp type started a conversation. While we chatted a very attractive young couple came in dressed in the mod style. Their clothes were fancy and expensive, but very untraditional. The girl wore a very short skirt and high boots, while the young man looked Edwardian. They were both pleasant and friendly, but Colonel Blimp was outraged by their appearance. His face got redder and redder, and he spluttered as he said, "Do you know whot you are?! You are f…ing bawstards, that's whot!" The young man turned to him and said, "And you, sir, are an offensive gentlemen." Colonel Blimp beat a spluttering retreat.

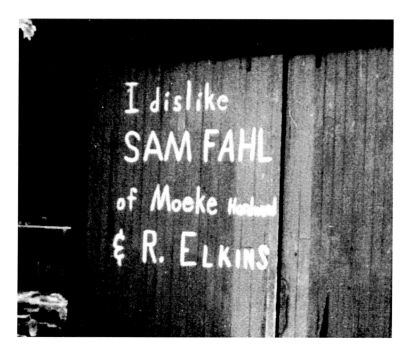

SAID LIKE A GENTLEMAN.

11 THE CONTINENT

Sweden

Most of us in international business spoke a few languages. Swedish was not usually one of them, but most Swedes spoke some English so it was easier to travel there than in some other countries.

Not all my free time was spent in Britain, where I was familiar with the fishing. Once, when I was to spend a weekend in Sweden, I wrote to the manager of Stockholm's elegant Grand Hotel for information. I gave him a list. I wanted to: (a) fish for trout, (b) in a stream, (c) with flies, and requested his guidance. On arrival, I asked for the manager, who came out quickly to greet me. "I received your letter," he said, "and have investigated. Unfortunately, at this time of the year there is absolutely no fishing in the archipelago." The archipelago is a group of islands in the Baltic Sea with: (a) no trout and (b) no stream, making (c) my flies worthless.

Undaunted, I found my way to a fly shop where by great luck I encountered three young Swedish men who were going trout fishing that weekend. They offered to be my guides, mainly so they could practice their English. Their trailer was laden with enough of the most delightful smorgasbord to make meals for the four of us for the entire weekend. The smorgasbord was excellent but my lodging was not. There was no room for me to sleep in the trailer so I slept in a Spartan youth hostel on a steel cot with no mattress. The hostel also didn't have running water. As if that weren't enough, I got skunked. But I did get to spend several hours watching an excellent Swedish caster make casts of over a hundred feet with a split cane rod and shooting head. It was poetry in motion and a pleasure to watch though not nearly as satisfying as the smorgasbord!

A German Joke

The manager of our German factory arranged for me to fish with a friend of his who maintained a stocked stream. I told my host that I would rather not keep any fish unless he would like some, since I could not cook them. He said he had plenty of fish, and so declined.

I caught a number of decent-size rainbows and quickly released them. Then I landed a sizable brown trout, and released it too. My host called me up short, yelling: "Nein, dummkopf! Dass war ein bachforelle!" ("No, dumb head! That was a native trout!") It was OK to release hatchery rainbows but not native brown trout, which were obviously too valuable to release, if we can figure out the logic or humor in that. Who knew? I believe it was Mark Twain who said German jokes were no laughing matter, but maybe he was not joking.

Putting on the Ritz

Dermot Wilson suggested I call on Charles Ritz at the Ritz Hotel in Paris. The history of the hotel is impressive: I imagined the spirits of Cesar Ritz, Coco Chanel, and Auguste Escoffier might be wandering the halls, and, of course, Ernest Hemingway, who "liberated" the hotel and the bar in 1945. Charles Ritz, the owner, was widely known as an expert Atlantic salmon angler and he befriended me. He knew I was fascinated by his fishing stories.

Charles was always delighted to have a drink with me and talk but whenever I invited him to dinner he declined, saying Madame Foy was expecting him. I did not know who she was and figured it was none of my business. I did get a clue, however, one day while waiting for Charles in the bar at the Ritz. The bartender and the only other customer appeared to disdain me. They made no effort to keep their conversation private, seeing I was an American and assuming I did not speak French. Wrong. They chatted at length about M. Charles and I'll never forget the punch line: "What a formidable man at age eighty to keep a forty-year-old woman happy!"

Charles wanted to take me to his casting pond on the roof of the hotel a couple of times but we were rained out on both occasions. He did show me some rods he had designed for Fenwick, however. His interest being primarily Atlantic salmon fishing, he liked to fish big rivers where he could make long casts. He had powerful arms and he designed the rods for powerful casters. I am not one of those casters, so the rods were not for the likes of me. I wonder how Madame Foy did with them.

*****

I had learned that St. Peter was the patron saint of fishermen, and during my travels I would look for a St. Peter's medal. Finally I found a source for the medal at the Sacré Coeur cathedral in Paris. I bought one as a keepsake and then decided to visit the huge crypt under the cathedral. It contained several large marble tombs and there were about twenty heavy metal doors around the circumference. A loud clanging of the doors heralded the evening closing of the crypt as one door after another slammed shut. I did not want to spend the night in a crypt among tombs of long-dead nobility and luckily I managed to get to an open door—one of only three that were still unlocked.

On the Way Home

On my way home from Europe I had to stop in New York to meet with our bankers to discuss an acquisition I was working on. I had a guaranteed reservation, at a guaranteed rate, at the Plaza Hotel.

My plane was late getting into New York, and when I arrived at the hotel's reception desk I was told they were full. It was late, I was tired, and I protested to no avail. They finally told me I could have a suite, but at a higher rate. I claimed a guaranteed rate was a guaranteed rate, but that also fell on deaf ears. I then told them not to concern themselves any further and, pointing to a sofa on the other side of the lobby, said, "I'll just sleep over there, no need to worry." So I plunked down my bags and fly rods and sat on the sofa, though I had no intention of sleeping there. In no time at all the manager approached me and said, "Please come with me, sir." He put me up in one of their corner suites at my guaranteed rate.

Maybe you remember the movie *The Great Gatsby* with Robert Redford and Mia Farrow. In the film they had a huge, luxurious corner suite at the Plaza, with a view of Central Park and Fifth Avenue. My suite was identical, and it may have even been the same one. In New York, chutzpah works.

THIS SIGN IS A DISGRACE,
EVEN IN THE BACKWOODS.

12 THE REVOLUTION IN FLY FISHING

Fly fishing started to change after World War II. It underwent a revolution around 1970.

THE POSTWAR YEARS

My perspective of fly fishing developed in the era following WWII. Veterans of that war drove practically all aspects of society in the United States for years. When I started college in 1949 most of the upperclassmen were veterans, and they wanted to make up for their war years by enjoying life to the max. Many of these vets began seeking out fly-fishing tackle and books from before the war. They absorbed the old techniques and tackle, then looked for new ideas and equipment.

New ideas came from Vince Marinaro, whose *A Modern Dry Fly Code* was published in 1950. Ernie Schwiebert's *Matching the Hatch* (1955) taught those who had some understanding of fly fishing what hatches were all about. It was a groundbreaker. Helen Shaw's *Fly Tying* (1970) taught people how to tie flies through step-by-step illustrated instructions, setting a new standard for clarity.

Bamboo Rods

Right after WWII, most anglers were still fishing with split bamboo rods that were made before the war. These rods required a lot of care and many of them were not easy to cast, although some of the better designs still find acceptance. Handcrafted rods by American makers such as Leonard, Orvis, Payne, Thomas, Young, Dickerson, Winston, Powell, Garrison, and Gillum were expensive but worth it, being carefully and beautifully made. Orvis and Leonard split cane rods, for example, sold for a little under $200, a princely sum in those days. Prized for their aesthetics, these prestigious brands retained some of the market share and many of my friends still enjoy fishing with split cane.

Inexpensive production cane rods made by Granger, South Bend, and Heddon were available in the price range of $12 to $25, but the shortage of cane and the advent of fiberglass pushed cane rods out of the market. Production cane rods cost about the same as fiberglass, but they were becoming scarce, and fiberglass soon replaced them.

My Best Hundred-Year-Old Friend

In 2007 Nancy and I moved to a retirement home, where I met a man twenty years my senior, Bill Martindill, who became a fast friend. He was ninety-eight years old at the time and came from the hills of southeastern Ohio, a few miles from where I had lived as a boy. I told him of my years working with Orvis and he told me about his history in fishing.

In 1945 the South Bend Tackle Co. was in trouble because bamboo rods were no longer selling well, and fiberglass rods had not yet become popular. Bill was named president of South Bend, and immediately went about the task of sorting out their problems. Bill soon saw that the market for inexpensive production cane rods was finished, so he called Wes Jordan of Orvis.

Wes Jordan had once been in charge of South Bend's rod business, and he was aware that the company had a very large supply of Tonkin cane, which Orvis could use and South Bend could not. Orvis bought the higher-quality cane, which tided them over until Tonkin cane again became available, and continues to make excellent cane rods. The rest of the cane was sold to a company that used it to make window shades.

Fiberglass Rods

Disruptions in shipping caused by the war cut off the sources of good cane. Later, the communist takeover of China in 1949 made good cane hard to come by, whether due to our regulations or those of the Chinese. These two factors practically killed the cane rod business and fiberglass rods rapidly took over their market share.

Most traditional anglers did not like the new fiberglass rods, partly because of their unfamiliar action, and partly because the traditionalists liked the fine appearance of nicely finished cane rods. However, fiberglass rods were much less expensive than cane rods, and they were actually easier to cast. Fiberglass soon dominated all tournament casting, as it improved both accuracy and distance.

Synthetic Fly Lines

Prior to the introduction of synthetic fly lines in the 1950s, silk was the most common material used for fly lines. Silk lines required extensive care, as they had to be dried, stretched, and coated with a dressing after every outing. Synthetic lines eliminated the need for all of that. Some anglers believed silk lines allowed for a more delicate presentation of the fly but most of us felt synthetic lines were a great deal because they were trouble free and much more practical.

Nylon leaders and tippets soon replaced silkworm gut. This was a big improvement, even though the early quality was poor compared to today's leaders.

It used to be that you bought a fly rod and guessed at the line size needed to balance it. Then, around 1965, the American Fishing Tackle Manufacturers Association developed a system of rating rods for line size. This made a huge difference since a line that balances the rod gives good casting action. By 1970 rod makers had adopted the system and began printing the recommended line size on their rods.

Fly-Fishing Organizations

A handful of elite fly-fishing clubs existed before the war in major cities such as New York, Chicago, and San Francisco, but the growth of fly fishing created broader-based clubs that played a vital role in its development. Trout Unlimited (est. 1959) and the Federation of Fly Fishers (est. 1965) both supported conservation and promoted fly fishing. They provided anglers all over the country with an opportunity to get together, hear lectures, and discuss fly fishing, thus supporting interest in the sport. Their mission continues to this day.

THE 1970S—BIRTH OF A REVOLUTION

The 1970s brought on a revolution in fly fishing. From a small, esoteric, elitist field it developed into a much broader industry, growing exponentially. There were new tackle products, new manufacturers, new books, new magazines, new organizations, new fly shops—all of which benefited the WWII vets and all the rest of us.

Major Factors in the Growth of Fly Fishing

Several new developments in the 1970s helped to create a boom in the fly-fishing industry, but five stand out in my mind as being revolutionary: 1) graphite rods, introduced by Fenwick; 2) better knowledge of fly hatches, provided through books such as *Selective Trout*; 3) the development of fly shops, such as those in the Orvis dealer program; 4) the distribution of books through fly shops by the Lyons Press; and 5) a larger market provided by a more affluent society.

Graphite Rods

One of the greatest developments in fly fishing was the graphite rod, introduced by Fenwick in 1973. By 1986, Fenwick's fly rod sales were 84 percent graphite. Although the new graphite rods were much more expensive than their fiberglass counterparts, their lightness, sensitivity, and quick recovery made most anglers willing to pay several times more for them than fiberglass. There have been continual incremental improvements in graphite rods ever since.

Fenwick dominated the graphite rod market for many years, but eventually Fenwick personnel founded Sage, and Fenwick faded from the scene. Orvis and Sage eventually came to dominate the market in quality graphite fly rods.

Graphite rods quickly replaced fiberglass in tournament casting, just as fiberglass had replaced bamboo.

Fly Reels

Fly reels have gradually improved through the years. In earlier times, reels were simply considered a means for storing line. The newer reels, however, became tools for fighting fish. One development was the addition of an exposed rim, which enabled the angler to control the running of the fish. The first such rims I can recall were introduced on a reel by Scientific Anglers and one by Orvis, with the fine CFO reel named in honor of Charles F. Orvis.

Then came the addition of disc drags, which could handle large game fish, both salt and freshwater. Large-arbor reels then gained prominence among trout reels as they require less pressure on the rim to put pressure on the fish. If the fish surges, it can run with less resistance from the reel and the angler can retrieve line more rapidly than with conventional reels.

Breathable Fabrics

The sporting goods industry began creating what we call "breathable" materials, probably best known under the Gore-Tex brand, in 1969. They allow water vapor to escape, but shed liquids.

Breathable waders and rain jackets were well received by anglers. Earlier waders, made of rubberized fabrics, were durable, but they were heavy and hot in warm weather, and not warm in cold weather. Breathables made fishing a lot more comfortable. Neoprene waders also filled a niche for cold-water fishing.

The Orvis Company Network
Leigh Perkins bought the Orvis Company in 1965 and started developing the modern system of marketing fly tackle by establishing a nationwide network of dealers, retail stores, lodges, outfitters, and fishing schools, most of which began after Leigh took over Orvis. The availability of guides and lodging drew many new anglers to the field. No matter how expert the angler, he could fish an unfamiliar stream with a guide and learn as much in one day as he could learn in many days fishing alone. Many independent dealers and guides were developed through the Orvis program.

New Books, and their Distribution through Fly Shops
In 1971 a new book, *Selective Trout*, by Doug Swisher and Carl Richards, created a breakthrough by making fly hatches understandable to the average angler. A more complete reference book, *Hatches*, by Al Caucci and Bob Nastase, followed in 1975, and provided more in-depth information on fly hatches. *Fly Tying* by Helen Shaw, published in 1979, was a great step forward in teaching understandable fly-tying techniques.

Publishers that focused on fly fishing were unheard of until *Selective Trout* and other new books made it possible for Nick Lyons Books to begin gathering a library of around three hundred titles. Nick realized that fly-fishing books would be better distributed through fly shops than bookstores. Frank Amato, another fly-fishing publisher, added to the list of available books, publishing new western writers.

Fly-Fishing Magazines
Public interest in fly fishing was increased when, in 1969, Don Zahner founded *Fly Fisherman Magazine*. *Fly Fisherman* provided cover-to-cover information on fly fishing. In addition to articles, it contained advertising that told anglers where they could purchase the products and books. John Randolph soon succeeded Zahner at *Fly Fisherman* and edited it for many years.

Later, John Merwin started *Fly Rod & Reel*. Silvio Calabi succeeded John, and both built it into a valuable resource. Before these magazines, we were lucky to find a single article on fly fishing in any of the older outdoor magazines.

A River Runs Through It

The movie *A River Runs Through It*, based on the book by Norman Maclean, premiered in 1992 and gave fly fishing a huge boost. It romanticized the sport—I mean, how could you make fishing more exciting other than by killing Brad Pitt after he caught one hell of a fish?

Nancy and I took our grandson, Jake, to see the movie when he was six. There is a scene where Paul (Brad Pitt) disappears under the water while playing a huge fish down a rapids. When Paul's arm appears above the water, holding a bent rod, Jake enthused, "He still has it on!" I knew then that he was a fisherman. Jake knew the bent rod meant Paul was still fighting the fish, and therefore all was well. (Unfortunately, Paul was later rubbed out by gamblers to whom he owed money.)

Maclean's 1976 book is excellent, and is a classic of fly-fishing literature, but it was the movie that moved the market.

THE DIVIDED HIGHWAY.

"You got to be careful if you don't know where you're going because you might not get there."—Yogi Berra

PART III: The Fly Shop, 1975–1985

13 A DIFFERENT ROAD

By early 1975 I was starting to believe two things: First, I was not going to progress in Toledo where I ended up when the glass company bought Aeroquip. Second, fly fishing might be a viable alternative. So should I continue in the international field? Up until then I had a goal of being international vice president of a major company.

Nancy's gift of a fly rod had opened my eyes to another world, and getting into fishing full-time had continuing appeal. The development of the Keel Fly had been interesting, but I couldn't see making a career out of a fly.

I'd like to think my thought processes were cerebral—that, like Robert Frost, I would carefully evaluate the possibilities and make a brilliant decision choosing the road less traveled by. It probably would make all the difference, as Frost said, but would it be a good difference?

I was a lousy fit at the glass company in Toledo. It should have been obvious immediately when a vice president informed me that even if my boss told me to do something wrong, I should do it. First, I should make him put it in writing. I had never operated that way, nor did I ever intend to. I would take my risks and my lumps. After a reasonable trial, I determined that I needed to seek other employment—I just did not fit there.

I decided to look for another job in international business. While searching I gave some thought to establishing a fly shop, but then an offer came along for just the kind of international job I had been seeking. I told them that though I believed we had agreed on terms, I would like to sleep on it. The president of the company suggested I have breakfast with them the next morning to conclude the deal. That evening, Nancy and I celebrated my good fortune.

The next morning, I got up and suddenly thought, "I can't do this. I've worked for three companies, learned their products, their accounting, their manufacturing, their advertising, their competition, and I don't want to go through all that again."

I had done enough investigating to have reached the conclusion that the opportunity to open a fly shop existed. Michigan had become my home fishing area, and it was the home of both Nancy's and my families. I figured the kind of shop we wanted should be in a city large enough to support it. Way back in college I had told Nancy that if I ever picked a city to live in based on its quality, it would be Grand Rapids. Since Grand Rapids was near good trout streams, that made it a good choice.

We picked Orvis as our number one supplier. I had visited several fly shops and concluded having one major supplier was the best arrangement. Only Orvis had the brand and the dealer program we needed.

We had only one child left at home, Andrea, and Nancy was looking for something to do. We decided to start the business together. We then counted our assets: I had $25,000 in my pension fund, which would be the capital for the store, and we had about the same amount of equity in our Toledo house, which would provide a down payment on a new house. It seems like slim pickings today, but that's all there was.

I called my prospective employer and said, "You'll hate me for this, but you would hate me more if I decided it later. I have decided to go into my own business."

I can't take credit for Robert Frost–quality thinking. I think it was more Yogi Berra type: "When you come to a fork in the road, take it."

That fork in the road led Nancy and me to an interesting and rewarding career running a fly shop. It also enabled us to get to know some fascinating people in the fly-fishing business. We were fortunate to be entering this industry during the fly-fishing revolution of the 1970s.

THAT WINDING ROAD STRAIGHTENS
OUT AFTER A FEW DRINKS.

14 LEIGH PERKINS & THE ORVIS COMPANY

Orvis' support was the most important factor in establishing Nancy's and my fly shop. And Leigh Perkins was the man who made Orvis an industry leader.

Leigh Perkins

As Leigh Perkins explained in his book, *A Sportsman's Life*, his mother was the niece of Mark Hanna, a ship's chandler from Cleveland who had earned a fortune and founded the Hanna Mining Company in Minnesota, a forerunner of the 3M corporation. He then became the campaign manager who took William McKinley to the presidency of the United States in a race run against the great orator William Jennings Bryan. Leigh came from a wealthy family and stated he did not have to work, but he loved to. On his own he built enough capital to purchase the Orvis Company at age thirty-seven.

Charles Orvis created the first mail-order catalog in the United States in 1856. The company introduced the first split bamboo rods in 1870 and introduced the ventilated spool fly reel in 1874. Much of their reputation later relied on the Mary Orvis Marbury book, *Favorite Flies and Their Histories*, published in 1892. Dudley "Duckie" Corkran bought the company from the Orvis family in 1939.

Leigh bought Orvis from Corkran in 1965 for $400,000. At the time it was a prestigious company, but quite small, with annual sales around $500,000. It didn't take long, however, for Leigh to build the company into the leading manufacturer and distributor of quality fly-fishing tackle in the world. The Orvis network grew to thirty-nine company-owned stores, over five hundred dealers, and ninety endorsed lodges and outfitters, plus a complete UK subsidiary. The company has since exceeded $300,000,000 in annual sales, sixty times as large as when Leigh bought it.

One of Orvis' major strengths was that Leigh and his sons, Perk and Dave, were skilled and avid anglers. *A Sportsman's Life* is an inspiring read for any outdoorsman, as well as any businessman. Leigh, Perk, and Dave knew their craft and their business.

The Orvis Company
By the time Nancy and I started the Thornapple Orvis Shop in 1975, Orvis had taken a huge leap forward by adding a complete line of graphite rods, making the company no longer dependent on the impregnated cane fly rods that had made it famous. Orvis was also large enough to gather and keep a spectacular staff.

The Orvis Company provided virtually all the products a dealer needed to survive. It had the products, the programs, and the name recognition a dealer needed. Orvis was the only supplier who could, single-handedly, provide a decent living to a dealer. Most suppliers were limited to one major product, such as rods, lines, waders, etc., and the last thing I wanted to do was spend my time evaluating the product lines of a whole bunch of different suppliers. Orvis offered the industry's most complete line of fly-fishing tackle. Once again I was associated with the industry leader, as I was with Caterpillar and Aeroquip.

Among the many advantages Orvis offered was a line of competitive fly rods, reels, lines, leaders, flies, gadgets, books, waders, and outdoor clothing that ranked high in the field. The company had an aggressive development program that kept it up to date in its product line along with the leading mail-order catalog in the fly-fishing industry. Dealers could advertise in the catalog as well as in the company newsletter and use its mailing list. High-quality Orvis-endorsed lodges and outfitters were listed in the catalog and later on the company website. Orvis was also known for contributing liberally to conservation organizations and projects.

Orvis also had company stores in larger urban markets. I was amazed when I first visited the Orvis company store in Manhattan. No other fly-fishing company had succeeded with a store in New York or any other major American city. Angler's Roost and William Mills, once important New York fly shops, had closed. Abercrombie & Fitch and Eddie Bauer stayed in business but dropped their fly-fishing departments.

Slow Down

Orvis business meetings were mainly for business, but we always fished a day or two afterwards at some of the most interesting fishing locations. These meetings produced a few choice stories as well. My favorite concerns Jimbo Meador, the sales rep from the Gulf Coast. Jimbo, who had the slowest, thickest drawl I ever heard, was hired to be Tom Hanks' voice coach for the movie *Forrest Gump*. You may remember the line, "My mama said life is like a box of chocolates." Jimbo taught Hanks to speak that way.

One day, at a trade show, Jimbo and I were trying to move a heavy display case. At one point I said, "Slow down, Jimbo." Jimbo laboriously drawled, "Sl-ow da-own? No-body e-vah said tha-at to me befo-ah." Jimbo was always able to add at least one syllable to just about any word, and sometimes more than one.

Grandpa Was the Boss

Leigh Perkins and I have grandsons about the same age, and we often swapped tales about the boys when we got together. Leigh once told me about the time his grandson Simon, at age seven, called the Orvis switchboard and asked to be put through to Grandpa. "Grandpa, I have a great idea," he said. "Let's go fishing. Pick me up at the house." Clunk, he hung up.

Leigh hastily rearranged his evening schedule, then headed over and found Simon waiting by the road with all his gear, ready to fish. They went to the Battenkill, spent the evening catching fish, and then headed home.

Leigh was quite surprised when they got home and found Simon's mother frantic. She had no idea they had gone fishing and turned the town upside-down trying to find Simon. Even the police were involved. She read the riot act not only to Simon, but also to Leigh. Simon said sheepishly, "I thought Grandpa was the boss." Leigh's reply was, "Not always."

THOSE ARE NOT DRY-FLY FISHERMEN, NO SIR!

> # FIRST GET THE FACTS
>
> ## LATER YOU CAN
> ## DISTORT THEM
> ## ALL YOU WANT

FROM PAPA JOE'S RESTAURANT IN ISLAMORADA

Sure beats arguing about hatches.

Smartass

One evening in early summer of 1985, I went fishing on the Battenkill River with some of the staff from Orvis. The fish were feeding on a hatch of yellow flies. I caught a specimen and realized I could not identify it so I put it in a plastic box and stuck it in my pocket. The next day at lunch with Leigh and the managers, I passed it around and asked if anyone knew what it was. Opinions were evenly divided. Some said it was a sulfur but others thought it was a cahill. It could not be either one, however, because the sulfur has three tails and this fly had two, and it had no wing markings like the cahill. Stymied!

That afternoon I went to the Orvis store, got a copy of Caucci and Nastase's *Hatches* off the bookshelf, and found the insect. It was *Epeorus vitrea*, not a common fly in Vermont, and unknown in Michigan. At dinner I explained what I had found: As a two-tailed yellow fly with no wing markings it had to be *Epeorus vitrea*, the only *Epeorus* species that time of year.

Leigh asked, "How in hell did you figure that out?" I replied, "Well, there is this fly-fishing company just down the road, and they sell books, and it was in one of those." I was tagged a smartass for that. The situation reminded me of one of my favorite signs I had found in Islamorada: "First get the facts, later you can distort them all you want."

Pale Morning Duns

Leigh owned access to a couple of spring creeks in the Star Valley of Wyoming a few miles south of Jackson Hole. He asked me to evaluate the insect population there en route to a day's fishing and dropped me off to do some nymph seining.

I was prepared for this task because several years earlier I had substituted mosquito netting for the open-weave netting on my landing net. The net was capable of not only landing fish, but also capturing insects, whether drifting on the bottom, on the surface, or in the air, and it could also be used to sweep the tops of bushes to collect bugs.

I was pleased to report to Leigh that he had a great population of one of the best flies in the West: the pale morning dun (PMD), genus *Ephemerella*, including both species, *infrequens* and *inermis*. I was lucky because those are two of the easiest species to identify. That same day I caught a twenty-three-inch rainbow on a PMD then got into the biggest bunch of mating midges I have ever seen, fishing with Leigh and Vern Bressler when the fishing went off the charts.

LOCATION, LOCATION, LOCATION!

15 THE FLY SHOP

When Nancy and I prepared to open our fly shop in 1975 we located an appropriate building in the little town of Ada, a suburb of Grand Rapids. It was just a shell of a building, not yet finished inside. My son Sam was a student in the building construction program at Michigan State and he went with me to plan the work necessary to open the shop. After a couple of hours he announced he was going to skip fall semester to finish the building. I didn't think he should take the time off, but he was adamant: "This is not negotiable. You can't do it without me." He was right. It takes a ton of work to transform a shell into a shop.

Before we were even open for business, a woman came into the shop. When I asked if I could help her, she replied, "No, I just want to see where I am going to have to go to see my husband."

Building a Business

Dermot Wilson's idea that rods had to be tried out came home to roost. It was vital to me that customers interested in a fly rod should be fitted to the rod and not just go by the blarney fed to them by a clerk.

We developed a procedure we called "rodfitting": We would take the client outside and have him try out rods with three different actions. We would then ask him which seemed easiest to cast, and if we agreed with his appraisal, we would have him try two or three other rods with actions similar to the one he liked best. The reason anyone likes a rod is because it feels good to cast. And the reason it feels good is that the rod loads and the cast straightens out behind the caster without his having to think about it.

We strongly urged our customers to be fitted with a rod as we knew they would be happier with a rod that fit. It usually takes about a half hour to properly fit a rod and it is worth it. There may have been other shops somewhere doing the same thing, but we did not know of any at that time.

If a customer could cast a rod effortlessly without thinking about technique we knew he would be happy when fishing. We later used the same concept in casting classes. Different people have different reflexes and respond to different actions. We got a lot of arguments from some who said it was all physics and everybody should cast the same way. Baloney. My teacher had been a world champion caster, and he and I were nothing alike in strength and reflexes. We were physically different. Should Ali have boxed like Frazier? Should Jean-Claude Killy have skied like Stein Ericson? Jean-Claude said the idea was preposterous.

Another principle we followed was to quiz the client to figure out what he really needed, even if he thought he knew what he wanted. Years before at Jim Deren's Angler's Roost in Manhattan, I overheard a clerk arguing with a customer about his choice of a certain fly. The clerk insisted the customer really wanted another. Instead of arguing with the customers, we offered a free fly to anyone who brought in a natural one. That way, we learned what was hatching and at the same time, educated the customer by showing him the appropriate flies for the hatch.

I had also heard salespeople refuse to tell customers how to get to their own personal favorite fishing spots. Funny, I thought our job was to get the customers to the best fishing spots with the best tackle, provided there was legal access. Service and helpful advice had to be the basis for a good fly shop.

We also had a program I called "creative selling." We were willing to put items on layaway without any deposit, and generally it worked well. But sometimes people would fail to pick things up even after our reminders. So on a slow afternoon I would put those items in my car, drive to the office of the customer, and deliver them in person. That may have been a little pushy, but we had our life's savings invested in the business. If the customer decided he was no longer interested, that was OK, but usually they went through with the purchase.

※ ※ ※ ※ ※

As time went by, we started to hold fly-fishing classes. A customer came in one day and told me he had really been inspired by a class I had given on collecting insects on the stream. He realized he would need a fine-mesh piece of cloth to make a collecting net and he hunted high and low in his house for the perfect sample. Finally, he found it: His wife had saved her wedding veil and a small piece cut out of it was exactly what he needed. He figured she didn't need the veil anymore, and he was probably right—unless she found out what he had done.

※ ※ ※ ※ ※

There were some slow afternoons in the shop during the early years so we tried various things to build the business. First we added more clothes and gifts. Among the gifts were prints of wildlife art, which we hung on the shop walls and made available for purchase. I remember a print we had by David Hagerbaumer called *Flight of the Passenger Pigeons*. One day a customer looked at it and said, "I killed tons of those things in my day." I'm sure he thought they were doves since passenger pigeons had been hunted to extinction.

A Family Affair

Nancy and I both loved to work in the store. She took over all of the administrative and accounting functions, so that left tackle sales, promotion, and classes to me. She also loved to sell and she outsold me in clothing and gifts.

One day we decided to spice things up by having a sales com-

PHILOSOPHY HAS REACHED THE SIDE ROADS.

petition. This left me with a major advantage since I was the one who sold the more expensive fishing tackle and hunting gear and most of the outdoors clothing, so I suggested I'd give her a handicap. Apparently that pushed the wrong women's lib button. She said, "Handicap nothing! I'll change the mix of the merchandise." So she added more outdoors art, clothing, and gifts to the inventory, and the sales grew. I added a few things, too, such as a canoe.

We then started the sales contest, which lasted one month. On the last day of the contest we were tied. Then one of "my" customers came in when I was busy and bought "my" canoe from Nancy, putting her ahead in the contest. Before day's end, however, I sold one of "her" wildlife paintings which made me the winner in the end.

■ ■ ■ ■ ■

A lot of people ask what it was like for Nancy and me to work together. Well, it was great! Our talents are very different and we complemented each other. Nancy turned out to be an excellent administrator, which left me free to sell, run classes, and promote the business. She ran the accounting and worked with a computer programmer to design a point-of-sale program for the store that integrated accounting, purchasing, and inventory, and she later sold this program to other dealers. Nancy could turn out a complete financial statement on the first working day of every month. She understood the business as well as I did, was very cheerful, and could sell very well. I think that if people had not wanted to pick my brain about fishing they would have preferred to deal with Nancy. If you have a good marriage, no one will be a more reliable partner than your spouse.

Even our young daughter got into the act. Andrea became the darling of the merchants in our small town. Her school bus would drop her off near the shop and she would then make the rounds and report to us on what all the other merchants were doing. She usually stopped first at the florist, who at the end of each day tossed the unused flowers in the dumpster. Andrea would take the discarded flowers and graciously present them to the other merchants. The florist eventually put an end to that.

Tag It!
Every retailer has to attach price tags to the merchandise, and you'd be surprised at how many types of tags and ways of attaching them there are. One common way to attach price tags to soft goods, such as clothing, is with a "shooter gun," which is a plastic gun with a needle to pierce the fabric and attach a nylon cord that holds a cardboard price tag. One shop owner we knew assigned a new young employee to put price tags on a shipment of waders. She did—by shooting the nylon cord through the toe of a boot on each pair of waders.

Regional Managers
When Orvis asked me to be a regional manager I said yes if Nancy and

A MARRIAGE MADE IN HEAVEN.

IF YOU OBJECT TO LOGGING
TRY USING PLASTIC TOILET PAPER

I DIDN'T CLAW MY WAY
TO THE TOP OF THE FOOD CHAIN
TO EAT VEGETABLES

Bumper stickers

I could do it as a team. Together, we went on to establish over twenty specialty fly shops, about fifteen of which are still in business ten to twenty years later. Our official title was Regional Business Managers. In addition to being sales representatives we had the job of finding and developing new dealers. Since we were dealers ourselves, we were in a position to help other dealers with every facet of the business, including picking a location, budgeting, accounting, promotion, and all the other tasks a business owner has.

A fly-fishing writer from Pennsylvania once attended one of our dealer fishing outings. After a few days, he said he was amazed at the caliber of the dealers. When I asked him why, he said he had met six dealers and they were all good fishermen, seemed to know their business, and were pleasant and courteous. "You must have a plan," he said. "What is it?"

I replied, "They have to be good fishermen, know their business, and be pleasant and courteous."

He quizzed me further. I told him we would only take applicants who would specialize in fly fishing. Specialization was vital. I then went on to tell him about a fly shop owner who asked to carry our product line with the proviso, "I just want a little, enough to get people into the store. I don't want to carry very much." I had to be frank with him: That was the worst sales pitch I'd ever heard. Needless to say, we did not sign him up.

■ ■ ■ ■ ■

Leigh Perkins, owner of Orvis, observed the principle: "The customer is always right." We added the old rule: "Honesty is the best policy." I never worked for or with a company that did not follow these tenets. I was surprised when a new employee asked if we expected him to be honest. He had quit his last job, he said, because his employer demanded that he cheat the customers. I never saw a departure from the policy of honesty at Caterpillar, Aeroquip, or Orvis. Our new employee was relieved to know that honesty was our policy as well.

Traffic

At an Orvis dealer meeting, a young dealer asked me, "Dick, do you like traffic?" (He was referring to browsers in the store.)

I said traffic was essential, but some types were better than others.

He replied, "I hate it. I just stare at them until they leave." I don't know, but doubt he stayed in business long.

THE LOCAL BARTENDER DID NOT WANT
TO TELL ME WHAT THIS WAS ABOUT.

16 CLERKS & CUSTOMERS

As in any venture, relating to people—whether employees or customers—was the key to success in our fly shop.

Clerk in a Fly Shop

I particularly enjoyed waiting on customers in the shop. One day, two young couples from southern Indiana walked into the store and were dazzled to find a "real" fly shop. Apparently, they had seen nothing like it in southern Indiana.

Many folks from the Ohio River valley speak with a heavy drawl—I understand it, as I once lived in the Ohio valley. These two couples had come up to see the motorcycle races (which took them about six syllables to say, and they pronounced "cycle" as *sahcle*), but they were fascinated by our store. They bought a copy of my first book, *Fish the Impossible Places*, and then were off to the races.

A few days later I got a call: "Dick, this is Jim from Indiana. Ah owe you an apology. Ah di'n't know you wrote thet book. Ah thought you was jest some clerk in a flah shop."

I enjoyed being just a clerk in a fly shop and told him no apologies were due. We always enjoyed their later visits when the races were on.

Probst—I Know Him

Local fishing clubs often look for lecturers. After I presented a slide show at a neighboring town one night, a bunch of us were standing around and chatting. One of the members commented that I had not mentioned that I had invented the Keel Fly. Another member, not quite getting the picture, said, "Yeah, the Keel Fly. It was invented by a guy named Probst—I know him."

The man then proceeded to tell the story at length, referring several times to "Probst." Finally, I tried to quietly tell him that there is no *r* in the name, that it is Pobst. He brushed me off and pushed me aside and continued to tell about how well he knew "Probst." Oh, well.

Nothing but Dardevles

One evening, at a cocktail party, a man approached me and said he had heard I was a fly fisherman. I asked him if he fly fished too. "Oh, absolutely," he replied. "I don't do anything but fly fishing."

I asked what flies he liked to use. His answer: "Only Dardevles—nothing but Dardevles!" Just about every angler knows the Dardevle is a famous old red-and-white-striped metal lure, and has nothing to do with flies.

The Amazon

Shortly after we opened the shop, Dave Hise joined our staff. He had worked in a fly shop in Ennis, Montana, but was originally from inner city Los Angeles. Both he and his mother were athletes. Dave won bronze in Junior Olympics weightlifting and was a counselor at Magic Johnson's and Bill Walton's basketball camps. He told us his mother set records in college in track and basketball, and was a competitive weightlifter.

In his youth, Dave liked to play basketball on city playgrounds. The summer before his junior year in high school, a tough guy came at him on the court for reasons he didn't recall. His mom jumped in front of the guy and made him aware that he had to go through her to get to Dave. Listening to him tell the story, we could only picture her as some sort of Amazon—I envisioned a female Hulk Hogan.

Dave got married, and his Amazon mother came for the wedding. She was slender, tall, stylish, and beautiful. Both Nancy and I did a double take. Amazons apparently aren't what they used to be.

Dave went on to own a shop in North Carolina.

Call Him "Sir"

Two of our guides, John Kluesing and Walt Grau, guided in Michigan in the spring and fall and then in Alaska in the summer. After they returned the first year, John told us about the dangers of grizzly bears and how guides carried strap-on shotguns for protection against them. He said that on one trip he heard a noise behind him while fishing, and turned around to find a big grizzly standing on a high bank.

Nancy asked John what he did. "Well, you talk to them," he said. "You always talk to them."

"What do you say?" she asked.

"It doesn't matter what you say," John replied, "but you always call them 'Sir.'"

Don't Choke

Nancy once said she thought I went into fly fishing because I hated to wear a tie. But it wasn't just that I hated to wear a tie—ties are bad for your health. The only explanation I can find for the five-year difference in the actuarial tables, why women live longer than men, is because men wear ties and slowly choke to death.

Michigan Is Really Weird

Once we started allowing ourselves some vacation time, I went to the Elk Creek Lodge in Colorado.

At our first dinner, I was talking with some of the other guests when the conversation turned to where we were from. When I said Michigan, a guy from Oregon chimed in, "I was in Michigan once. It's

Maybe Michigan is weird.

Bathing Madonnas are now rare.

really weird." Someone asked what was weird about it, and Oregon replied, "Everybody has a statue of the Madonna in a bathtub in his yard, and they feed carrots to the deer."

Those things do occur but I had trouble thinking they represented mainstream Michigan habits. These days it's hard to find even one of those bathing Madonnas.

Insectual Viewing

Although we did not have a perfect record at the fly shop, we didn't believe in chasing customers away. For example, a microscope could be helpful to an angler wanting to study the fly hatches. Most microscopes are fairly expensive, so I was thrilled when we found one retailing for $60. Of course, it was not a traditional microscope. It was just a bunch of rubber fixtures into which you could insert combinations of lenses.

Glen Blackwood, our sales manager, was determined to sell a bunch of those microscopes. One day a nicely dressed young matron entered the store, wearing heels, a beige suit, and one of those fur pieces that go over the shoulders. She did not look like a customer for a microscope or any fishing tackle for that matter. That didn't stop Glen, however, who zeroed in on her and pitched that microscope for all he was worth. She kept rebuffing him and finally flounced toward the door. "Ma'am," Glen said, giving it one last try, "this is the best device ever made for insectual viewing." No sale. I lectured him on the techniques for sizing up a customer, but was privately cracking up.

Merry Christmas

The Christmas after my mother-in-law died we decided to honor her with the "Esther Stewart Memorial Christmas Tree," which we placed on the front porch of the store, complete with white lights. A few days later it was stolen—tree stand, lights, and tree together.

Disrespect for both my mother-in-law and the Christmas tree was too much. I was ticked. So I got a new tree and lights, nailed the stand to the porch, and completed the installation with a wrapping of extra-springy barbed wire from the tree stand up around the trunk. Our insurance agent was appalled. We were sure to get into trouble.

The very next day we found the tree knocked over, but the miscreant had obviously given up when he realized it would be quite a job to untangle the barbed wire. We resurrected the tree, and nobody ever tried to steal it again. For a while I toyed with the idea of marketing "New and Improved Christmas Trees" with barbed wire already wrapped around the trunk, but decided the market was much too limited. Merry Christmas!

Bottomed Out

During one our first Christmas seasons, Ed Frey, the chairman of the bank that financed our initial venture, came into the store. He ordered a number of gifts, enough to make our Christmas season a barnburner.

Next door, our landlord was building a new restaurant, and the construction site was a muddy mess. About a week before Christmas, Ed drove out to pick up his order and plowed right into the mud, bottoming out his big Cadillac to the axles. He came into the store fuming and sputtering, and I got an earful of what I could do with the stuff he had ordered.

I said, "Ed, we don't have anything to do with that construction job. I think you need to speak to the manager of the project."

"Who is that?" he asked.

"Ted Frey (his son)"

"Oh."

We called the towing company. They hauled the Cadillac out of the mud, and we cheerfully loaded his purchases into the car.

What Kind of Father Are You?

Busy as we were with the Christmas rush, I had a teacher conference to attend at my daughter's school. Andrea was our third child, about nine years old.

"What kind of father are you?!" challenged the teacher when

we sat down for the conference. I was flummoxed. I finally learned that the teacher's reaction related to my taking Andrea on her first trout-fishing trip (during which I was always close enough to help her, while giving her room to cast), which my daughter described in the essay on the following page.

■ ■ ■ ■ ■

Parenting requires special skills. Once, during the Christmas season, a woman with two rambunctious young boys visited the shop. She decided the shopping was over and proceeded to usher the boys out the door. On their way out we heard her say, "Now, we're going in the store next door, and there will be no stabbing!"

one time
there was a man
Who had a kid
he said to his
kid its time you
learn to wade
his kid said ok
and went to go
wading and the
kids Father said
go all the way
across and back
while the kid
was going acros
his father had
a phone call

and he left
his kid alone
in the stream
the kid fell
in and died
well the man
came out and
saw that his
kid was gone
he laghed
and said he
probly went up
stream that night
when the man
whent to bed

he heard a
noise like this
clonk clonk clank
then he hear
a voice say
your kid is dead
so said the ma
if you do not
care then you
will die do
oh yes I do care
about myk'd
good
now
say your prayrs
and go to bed

the end
moral
never leave
your kid
alone wnoh
learning to
wade

WHAT KIND OF FATHER ARE YOU?

17 NICK LYONS & THE LYONS PRESS

Fly-fishing books were a vital part of our business at the shop. We sold the books, and they helped attract browsers. I wish I had a nickel for every time a customer came into the shop and headed directly toward the bookshelves.

Nick Lyons is unquestionably the leader when it comes to fly-fishing books. His company, the Lyons Press, published or republished over three hundred fly-fishing books, including most of the best-selling books in the field. Starting about 1965, those books were of major importance in educating and entertaining anglers. The Lyons Press published under several imprints over the years and was ultimately sold to Globe Pequot Press, which still runs it.

Nick was born and raised in New York and he learned to fish on New York streams, mostly in the Catskills. He attended the University of Pennsylvania, graduating with a BS in economics, and fished Pennsylvania streams. He then earned his MA and PhD at the University of Michigan in American literature. While there, he fished Michigan streams. Nick was totally devoted to fishing, writing, teaching, and publishing. He later fished in the Rockies, writing his favorite among his own books, *Spring Creek*.

I first heard of Nick when he was an editor at Crown Publishers in New York City, where he worked from 1964 to 1980. He was also a professor at Hunter College from 1961 to 1987. For most mortals either would be considered a full-time job. On top of this he also wrote numerous books and articles.

I had to wonder how anyone could do so much. The answer was that he worked ungodly hours, typically getting up at 6:30 a.m. and working until 2:00 a.m. He could not support his family in New York any other way, and he was so devoted to writing and publishing that he could not quit until he founded his own company.

At Crown he created a series of about fifty-five sporting titles, both reprints and new books and mostly about fly fishing, under the trade name Sportsmen's Classics. These included such prewar classics as *A Book of Trout Flies* by Preston Jennings, *Trout on a Fly* by Lee Wulff, and *The Wonderful World* of Trout by Charlie Fox. While these books were considered classics and were written by highly respected anglers, they were mainly fishing stories and did little to improve the state of the art of fly fishing.

After World War II new books were produced that helped anglers begin to better understand flies and fly hatches, and Nick published or republished many of them. Perhaps the earliest of import were *A Modern Dry Fly Code* and *In the Ring of the Rise*, both by Vince Marinaro; *Streamside Guide* by Art Flick; and *Matching the Hatch* by Ernie Schwiebert, which was a big step forward in making angling understandable.

While at Crown Nick realized that a new method of distribution was needed if fly-fishing books were to sell well. He began to contact fly shops, which were becoming plentiful by 1970, as potential outlets as well as fly-fishing companies that published catalogs. Until that time, even the best books sold poorly. Nick's innovation was part of a groundswell of advances in fly fishing. Better books, better distribution, and better tackle all reinforced each other.

In 1971 *Selective Trout* by Carl Richards and Doug Swisher provided the impetus to get Nick's plan going. It made fishing the hatches understandable and appealed to the great mass of anglers—not just fly fishermen, but also converts from other types of fishing. Author Ernie Schwiebert once told me that his *Matching the Hatch* was probably the best-selling fly-fishing book up to about 1970, having sold twenty thousand copies. In contrast, by 1975 *Selective Trout* had sold a quarter million copies and was still going strong. That great book and Nick's marketing efforts made a big difference. Nick's fly-fishing books were a significant part of our shop's sales. We carried as many as fifty titles at a time, mostly two or three copies of each, but we would stock as many as a dozen copies of best sellers such as *Selective Trout*.

Nick founded Nick Lyons Books around 1980 and took the Sportsmen's Classics titles to the new company. Over time, this company morphed into the Lyons Press, with around three hundred fly-fishing titles, most of which were sold through fly shops and catalogs and a few distributors. These titles included several more books by Swisher and Richards, and many others by major authors such as Lefty Kreh, Dave Whitlock, and Tom Rosenbauer.

Nick wrote around twenty fishing books of his own, along with hundreds of articles for magazines, and ghost wrote a number of books. I envy Nick's fishing prose. I admire those who can capture the beauty of the trout stream in writing. In *Spring Creek* he wrote about fighting a good fish so convincingly, I almost felt I caught it myself:

I slapped the water a bit hard with the line and the fish made a terrific swirl and fuss at the surface and disappeared.

That did it, I thought. Gone. For the next week, minimum. I was ready for the hopper.

But for some reason I decided to wait, to play out this hand however long it took. I sat and fussed with my leader; I greased the braided butt slowly so it would not spritz on the surface, and I tied on still a longer tippet, remaking the knot twice. I watched the place where the bend riffle became flat and I kept glancing down at the slack water near my inside perch, looking for new insects.

Sure enough, fifteen minutes later, the old fellow was back, pressing his snout up boldly as ever, thumbing his nose at me. Or perhaps he just couldn't help eating, an itch I knew well. The sky was darker now, the wind chilly, and the worse weather made me think the Baetis might get stronger. So I rummaged in my busy vest and came up with a little tin box of #20 dark-olive Sparkle Duns. Well, that would round out everything I'd seen on the water, anyway.

On my first cast with the dark olive, the fly lit, floated a foot, came into the area where the fish was feeding, hesitated, and then the snout came up, swirled—to my fly or a real one next to it?—I struck, and the fish bolted upstream in a manic rush. I raised the rod high, wound hard to get the fish on the reel, and then stood and high-stepped upstream as the fish headed around the bend and into the heavy run that led into it.

It was a long fight, with edgy moments as the fish went farther upriver, then sulked in the belly of the pool, then made—too late—a few runs below me. The 6X held, the fish began to tire. I backed toward my spot on the bank, sat down, and eased the great fish closer.

Wow!

I'LL BUY THAT.

18 NIGHT FISHING IN MICHIGAN

As friends introduced me to fishing more of the hatches, many of them told me that the best hatches and fishing in Michigan were at night. Tales abounded, with a modicum of exaggeration, of the hawgs you could catch at night, though they usually left out that sometimes you got skunked. And there were certain places you just had to fish. I had a lot to learn, so I went where invited, and that took me to most of Michigan's best rivers.

The hardest part of night fishing is explaining to people why you do it and to convince them—and sometimes yourself—that you are having fun.

The Manistee River

When Nancy and I started the store we worked long hours. I had time to fish two evenings a week but only on the nearby Rogue River. The Rogue has great fly hatches but I yearned to fish other rivers as well.

For two years we had no full days off and no vacation, but we had fun anyway, working and building our business. Our first summer a customer came in and said that the night before he had really good luck during the Hex hatch on the Manistee. I had to go. Hex is short for *Hexagenia*, a huge mayfly that brings up the biggest fish, always at night. I begged off work then got in the car to begin the three-hour drive to the Manistee in the center of Michigan's Lower Peninsula.

I arrived at the river in the early evening and found there was no one in my favorite spot. I ate a sandwich and waited for dark and the huge hatch. It was a warm, muggy evening, sunny and pleasant, just the way you want it. I expected the hatch around 10:30 p.m. About 9:30 the wind came up, and I saw ominous clouds in the west. By 10:30 the wind was raging, the sky was black, and then it got cold. The hatch was killed and I drove home late, skunked. Sadly, I didn't get away for the Hex hatch again until the following year.

The Au Sable River

The Au Sable is the most famous trout stream in Michigan, and it has earned its reputation. This beautiful, rich stream in the center of the state has three main branches, terrific hatches, a great trout population, and spectacular trout cover under the cedar sweepers. It has gentle currents and is easy to wade, or you can enjoy floating in an Au Sable longboat, a long, shallow draft boat controlled by a guide with a pole.

The Au Sable is rich in all the night hatches, in addition to all the important daytime hatches. Most of us who fish it are well acquainted with the joys and jeopardies of fishing in the deep, dark night woods. A cedar swamp at night is almost completely devoid of any light because the dense branches cut it out. Even in the daytime, it is dark and you have to stay on the path or you will find it hard slogging. Once in the stream you get a little light from the night sky.

One night a good friend, Bob Walker, and I were determined to fish the great Hex hatch on a lower stretch of the Au Sable. The staff at the Gates Au Sable Lodge said it might be good. I was not familiar with that stretch, but it was near Bob's cabin, and he knew it well.

I carefully checked all three flashlights in my vest, preparing for the trip. All of them worked. I then drove to Bob's cabin, where we enjoyed dinner before heading to the stream. We would always go early to get familiar with the water before hatch time.

Bob led me through the dense cedar swamp. We got to the spot, and he left me near the path. He then went around the bend, where he was in easy calling distance just across a twenty-five-foot-wide peninsula. We chatted back and forth as we prepared for darkness and the hatch, and confirmed we would use our whistles as follows: One blast meant duns hatching. Two blasts meant spinners on the water. Three blasts meant trouble—the international distress signal.

It got dark, and I was blanked. After changing flies a couple of times, my flashlight burned out. No problem, I thought. I had two more.

I usually expect Hexes around 10:30 at night, but by midnight we had seen nothing. I decided it was a bust and time to go. "Bob," I called. No reply. I raised my voice, "Bob!" Nothing. I shouted. Noth-

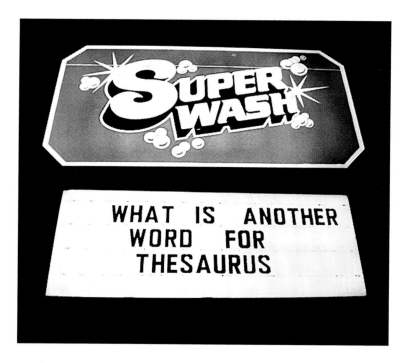

GEE . . . MAYBE . . . BRONTOSAURUS?

ing. I blew the whistle three times. Nothing. I was alone in the dark in unfamiliar territory.

About that time, my second flashlight burned out. No problem. I had another one. I started toward the path, and in a few minutes the third light burned out.

I knew I could not find my way in the swamp without light, so I decided to wade down the stream. I knew that even on the darkest night, I could see the sky and the silhouette of the treetops, and so find my way. The river would take me to the landing where my car was parked. But there was a catch: The water was about chest deep and the bottom of the stream was laced with logs from the old logging days. I had to feel for logs at every step, then feel the back side of each log with my foot and make sure I was on the bottom, then feel for the next log. It would take all night to reach the landing.

I changed my mind and decided to go to the spot where we had entered the stream and wait, either for Bob or for sunrise. I whistled again, just in case. No answer. After a while I saw a light coming through the swamp—no voice, just a light that approached slowly, coming closer and closer. Soon I could see Bob's face. He thrust a flashlight at me without a word and turned back toward the car.

Bob had come down with food poisoning earlier that night. He was in misery and had headed back to the car. Having no keys, he lay on the hood of the car until he could muster enough energy to respond to my whistles and bring me the light. I had to half-carry him to his bed when we got to the cabin. Fortunately, he recovered by morning.

Oh yes, what about my flashlights? I had tested them all, but the batteries were old, left over from the year before with only seconds of life left. Stupid! If two wrongs do not make a right, it's obvious three wrongs cannot possibly be any better. This is not the only scary night-fishing story I have, but it is enough. Bad trips are often more memorable than the good ones.

■ ■ ■ ■ ■

Rusty Gates was the owner of Gates Au Sable Lodge and founder and president of the Anglers of the Au Sable, a conservation group that has fought and won many battles to protect the river. He died too young, and will be missed for a long time. Rusty's father, Cal Gates, started the lodge in 1970. It was the first major fly-fishing lodge in the Midwest, and has created a standard of excellence for the area. I always stop at Gates for a report before fishing the Au Sable.

The Boardman

Carl Richards taught me that fish can be as selective in the middle of the night as they are in the daytime. It is hard to believe, but true.

To test this, you must be on a dark stream far removed from the lights of civilization. Look up and silhouette your hand against the sky, and you will see your hand clearly, distinguishing each finger. The trout can tell a dun from a spinner, or a Hex from a brown drake, very easily. I clearly remember one example of selectivity on a stretch of the Boardman River that runs through the center of Traverse City, Michigan.

The Boardman is a small river with good hatches. Its major claim to fame is that it is where the Adams dry fly was developed and inaugurated. Anglers have different ideas about what the Adams represents but it was a good general-purpose fly in the days before there was so much fishing pressure that the trout got super-selective.

It was on the Boardman that I got my greatest lesson in selectivity. It was a midsummer evening, when the big drakes hatch. I was well prepared with brown drake and Hex patterns, both duns and spinners. After wading up and down the river in waning daylight, I settled into my chosen spot. The evening went something like this:

9:30   Brown drake duns hatched and I caught a number of fish on duns until;

10:00   The fish still fed but not on my duns. A spinner took fish until;

ARE YOU LAUGHING YET?

10:30	The fish kept feeding but not on my drakes. Hex duns then took fish until;
11:00	The fish kept feeding but I had to switch to Hex spinners. Caught more fish until;
12:00	Rises got sparse and I went home.

I had a whole evening of great fishing. But if I had not been aware of how selective trout could be at night and kept on fishing the first fly I tied on, I'd have had half an hour of great fishing.

It was a terrific night until I left my favorite rod and reel on top of the car and drove away. It fell off. When I went back in the morning it wasn't there. For all the funny things that have happened in my years of fishing, this was not one of them.

The Pere Marquette River

During the 1980s a couple of young guides were becoming well known on the Pere Marquette, and I suggested they start a fishing lodge there. Jim and Tom Johnson had bought some old cabins on the river, and their location was ideal for a lodge.

Jim and Tom started the lodge, and they were busy almost from the beginning. The Pere Marquette has fine summer fly fishing, but the heaviest traffic is for the salmon fishing in the fall and the steelhead fishing in the spring. Their Pere Marquette River Lodge became the most popular salmon and steelhead fly-fishing destination in the Midwest.

Jim and Tom taught me some of the ins and outs of the gray drake hatch. For many years this hatch was only well known on the Pere Marquette, which runs into Lake Michigan south of the Manistee. The hatch there is of major proportions. It actually consists of three different species of the same genus, *Siphlonurus*. The three overlap, so the hatch lasts about a month. The mating activity is so heavy on the Pere Marquette, you can't possibly miss it. The Pere Marquette lodge still exists, so now I fish the gray drake with the new owner, Frank Willetts.

The gray drake actually exists on most trout rivers east of the Mississippi. The reason it was not widely known until recently is that the spinners don't usually show up until dusk or dark. The insects are practically invisible unless you stand in the riffles and look straight up in the air to see the drakes silhouetted against the sky.

After several years of fishing the gray drake hatch it occurred to me that while I had easily seen tens of thousands of spinners, I had hardly seen any duns or nymphs—I could have counted them on both hands. Before the mating swarm, tree trunks and cottages would be covered with the spinners so thickly, they appeared fur-covered. Everybody, including anglers from the East, agreed the hatch was a mystery.

Fly Rod & Reel magazine printed an article of mine on the gray drake hatch, titled "The Phantom Hatch." The editor and I thought it would be easy to figure out where the immature bugs were and I was confident we could have a follow-up article in a year or two.

I started a campaign to figure the hatch out. I called on every writer, guide, and fisherman I could think of to help. There were many suggestions as to how we could find the immature insects but none checked out. After a few years of no success, I offered a $100 reward to anyone who could solve the riddle. I took a lot of ribbing since I was supposed to know a thing or two about aquatic insects. My friends couldn't believe I had not come up with answers.

After ten years of wading through swamps and up spring creeks, climbing over log jams, I had no luck. Neither did the writers, guides, or fishermen—the $100 reward offer produced nothing. Then a very talented guide named John Miller moved to Michigan and solved the problem in one season. The secret was that the nymphs migrated long distances to swim in swamps, backwater eddies, and oxbows. They were living in shallow water among the rushes and grasses, and swam so fast they looked like minnows. You had to be very quick with a long-handled net to catch them.

John captured large numbers of the gray drake nymphs, hatched them in aquariums, and photographed them in digital format. Not

ANOTHER MARRIAGE MADE IN HEAVEN.

only did he win the $100 reward, but also got a contract to provide the photos for my revised book on mayflies.

■ ■ ■ ■ ■

You may have heard anglers say, "The air was full of spinners, but it got dark and cold and they went away." That is only part of the story. A major reason the flies went away is that the swarm is usually all male and if the females don't show up, they are not going to hang around all night. No mating, no fishing. You could say the mating swarm is like a singles bar—the drakes circulate for a while, and if they don't hook up, they head for home.

Halfway through the gray drake spinner fall the fish will often continue to feed but ignore your artificial fly. If you go one size larger they will often resume taking your fly. I believe the fish will take the larger fly because it stands out from many smaller flies but still does not look totally strange.

■ ■ ■ ■ ■

One evening after fishing the gray drakes, Jim Johnson and I were shooting the bull and got to discussing the Ten Commandments. I thought it was strange that an old man could convince people he had come down from the mountain with two stone tablets containing the word of God. Jim's reply was, "How do you think people would have reacted if he said, 'Look at these neat rules I carved in stone up on the mountain'?" I had no good answer for that.

The Rapid River

Invited to fish the Rapid, a small Michigan river east of Traverse City known for its Hex hatch, I drove to the designated meeting place. I asked my host, Kelly Galloup, questions about what to expect that evening: Would there be duns, or spinners, or both? "Oh, only spinners—there aren't any duns," he replied. Having spinners without duns would be miraculous, sort of like a reenactment of the Immaculate Conception.

Around 10:30 at night the spinners started bumping into us as they flew upriver. Kelly was right. There were no duns, at least not

PRICEY FOR THE NORTH WOODS
BUT OK BY SPITZER STANDARDS.

where we were. I couldn't rest until I figured out why. I could never resist a quandary related to fly hatches.

It took me a couple of years to find the answer. The Rapid River had a strong current, and it swept the stream free of silt. All the silt collected downstream in the delta where the river entered a lake. The eggs hatched in the river's riffles, and the nymphs then migrated down to the delta. At hatch time, the flies hatched out of the silt and mated nearby, then the females flew upstream to lay their eggs in the oxygenated riffles.

I studied two other rivers that had little silt but huge deltas downstream. I then drove the roads up the rivers and clocked the distance from the delta to the middle of the egg-laying riffles. The average on all three rivers was three miles. This explains why Kelly had never seen duns on his river.

The Muskegon River

The Muskegon was hardly fished by fly anglers when I first moved to Michigan. It is only forty-five minutes north of Grand Rapids, but few people knew how to fish it with flies. There were lots of fish and lots of insects, but they were mainly caddisflies. Sometimes we got lucky and caught good, fat fish on the Muskegon, but we couldn't figure out how to take them consistently.

Part of the problem was that Gary LaFontaine's *Caddisflies* listed 193 species of caddis, and we had no idea which ones were hatching. After some years of spotty fortune, Carl Richards and I decided we had to figure it out, so we seined caddis larvae in quantity and sent them to Michigan State. We asked them to tell us what the larvae were, but only the really predominant ones. It turned out there were only two significant caddisflies in the Muskegon River, both of family *Hydropsychidae*.

Carl started to spend two or three nights a week camped out on the river, fishing and trapping bugs at all hours of the night. That process eventually led to our producing the book now known as *The Orvis Vest Pocket Guide to Caddisflies*.

■ ■ ■ ■ ■

At first, to get to the Muskegon, Carl and I followed a path along a power line to the point where a couple of wires headed across the river. We would then go down a high, steep bank that we called "heart attack hill" because of the fun we had getting back up in the middle of the night after hours of fishing. For a long time that was our favorite place to fish.

I had one experience there that was very instructive. Late in the evening the fish kept rising, but got extremely selective. They were taking spent caddisflies, and only in very slow water. We were seldom able to connect, however, until I discovered that we had to use what I call an "anticipation strike." If you wait until the fish rises, you will not set the hook. You have to watch for the rise, mark the location, then cast to that spot and set the hook when the fly gets to the site of the rise, before the fish rises. You have to set the hook in anticipation of the strike. Too soon, or too late, is too bad. I explained this to my young grandson one evening, and he was soon catching fish regularly.

■ ■ ■ ■ ■

One afternoon, while Carl and I were browsing in Rusty Gates' shop on the Au Sable, Rusty asked me, "Is the Muskegon really as tough fishing as they say?" I replied, "Rusty, the fish on the Muskegon are as selective at night as the fish on the Henry's Fork are in the daytime." Rusty raised his eyebrows in exaggerated skepticism, but Carl chimed in, "He's dead right!"

The Platte River

George Denny, an outdoors writer from Indianapolis, wrote a delightful book called *The Dread Fishwish*. George defined the fishwish as a psychoneurosis that afflicts anglers before the opening of trout season—the fisherman is a basket case of angst, waiting for the opening day.

George and I both vacationed in Leland in northwestern Michigan, and we got together several times to fish the Platte during the Hex hatch at night. George would always wear his favorite fishing hat, which he had spotted and picked up off the street during the Depression. He cherished that hat.

One night while we were fishing, George's beloved hat fell off and floated downstream into the darkness, irretrievable. He was upset until I convinced him this was equivalent to a burial at sea. It was a fitting end for the hat and one that the angler himself might aspire to.

The Little Squirrel

George Denny told me a story about the famous Indiana poet James Whitcomb Riley, who retired to his Indiana hometown and supposedly gave up writing and speaking, then was constantly badgered to give speeches at every public event in town. He announced he would not do any more, but people would invite him as the honored guest, promise him there would be no speeches, and then call on him to speak. Anticipating this, he showed up at a dinner and when called on to "say a few words," he said he had not prepared a speech but wanted to share a short poem he had thought of that morning:

> The higher the little squirrel climbs the tree,
> The smaller his asshole seems to be.

Riley then bowed, turned, and made his way slowly from the banquet hall.

The Jordan River

Nancy decided to visit an aged aunt near the Jordan, a small river near Charlevoix, Michigan, which I don't get to fish as much as I'd like. Now, maiden aunts are not known as great sources of fishing information, but I had no other. "Aunt," I asked, "Do you know anyone who really knows the fishing on the Jordan?"

"Why, yes," she replied. "Reverend Jones is eighty-six years old and has been fishing it all his life. He lives down there in that brown cottage." So off I hopped toward the brown cottage.

"I do know about the big mayfly hatch on the Jordan," stated the reverend. "You go down to Boyne Falls, turn left toward East Jordan, then south toward Deer Lake. Just at the south end of Deer Lake, you turn left on a dirt road and go to the end of that road. There is a trash can there. Take the path at the side of the trash can. When you reach the river, fish the upstream pool after dark."

Well, I did what the good reverend said, wondering what sort of wild goose I was chasing. Just as it got dead dark the fish started to rise. Three times I laid a Hex dun just up from the ring in the water. Perfect drifts they were, but no take. I switched to a Hex spinner and the fish grabbed on the first float. I landed it after a few minutes—a nice, well-marked brown just shy of twenty inches.

The old reverend made my evening, and I went home full of thanks.

Back to the Manistee

The Manistee River starts in the same part of central Michigan as the Au Sable, but the Manistee runs west into Lake Michigan, whereas the Au Sable is the only major river that goes east into Lake Huron.

Gas stations are important when night fishing—and not just to get gas. In the daytime you can seine for nymphs, but at night, go to a gas station where the flies have been attracted to the lights. You can then tell if duns are hatching or spinners are mating. If you see duns they will have just hatched. If you see spinners they will be laying eggs. Then all you have to do is head for the nearest river.

Another thing to look for while night fishing is that if light cahills are on the water, they will stop hatching around dark, but if you wait a while Hexes are likely to start hatching. Night fishing gets to be second nature with experience. You develop night vision and grow accustomed to the dark. You learn to take cues from ripples on the water and listen for slurping sounds in the dark shadows along the banks.

Three of us, George, Eric, and I, went fishing one night during the Hex hatch. We had checked the lights at the gas station and determined the hatch was in progress, and then decided where to fish.

I tripped and fell in the water just about dark but it was still a good while before Hex time, so I waded to the bridge where we had parked the car. The way George, a cardiac surgeon, tells the story, he found me at the bridge, shivering, blue-lipped, and nearly hypothermic, and determined we needed to go to the cabin to get me dry and warm. He says I looked up into the night sky and said, "We can't leave now, George. The Hex hatch is just starting."

Eric said my response demonstrated the tenacious determination of the Hex hatch angler. The way I saw it, I was wet and it was time to fish, so we did. You can't let a little chill interfere with the fishing. That's what it's like if you fish at night.

WHAT'S WRONG WITH DRY
CHILDREN IN ARKANSAS?

19 STEELHEAD & SALMON

Pacific salmon were introduced into the Great Lakes not long before Nancy and I started our shop in 1975. At the same time efforts were being made to improve the steelhead population. This involved trying to eradicate sea lamprey which preyed on the salmon, steelhead, and lake trout.

It was remarkable that the salmon, which included mainly chinooks and cohos, could adapt to the freshwater of the Great Lakes, since they came from the Pacific Ocean. There were many differences in the diverse habitats and new techniques had to be developed for fishing for both the salmon and the steelhead.

During their spawning runs up rivers steelhead and salmon provide fly-fishing opportunities of a different sort from trout. Our natural resources department told us that Michigan had bigger steelhead and salmon runs than the West Coast, but this probably meant only Washington, Oregon, and California. If the runs of British Columbia and Alaska were combined the total would certainly seem to be greater than Michigan's runs.

Practically everyone had once believed that the fish did not eat during their spawning runs in the rivers, but we now know steelhead do eat but Pacific salmon do not. The salmon's stomachs atrophy after entering the river and they die after one spawning run. I asked author Ernie Schwiebert why that was, and he told me that in Alaska the streams do not hold enough food for the salmon. Once they spawn, their eggs and progeny provide a food source for the steelhead. Ernie's opinion was based on the fact he was retained by Alaska for a number of years to study and improve their fishery.

Steelhead

I was not aware that anyone in Michigan knew that steelhead fed when on spawning runs, until one day when Dick Smith, one of my most knowledgeable outdoors friends, walked into our shop.

Dick told me the steelhead were feeding on stonefly nymphs. He may not have been the first person who figured out that steelhead feed in the river, but he was the first I ever knew. I found out he was right when I tried fishing with stonefly nymphs.

Our experience with steelhead in Michigan may differ from the West Coast experience. It appears to me from my sparse information that the tendency to use bright attractor flies in the West could be due to the larger rivers and more sparse fish populations. In Michigan we fish almost exclusively with dead-drifted natural-color flies. The population densities in our smaller rivers may be a reason why steelhead feed selectively on natural insects or eggs and seldom chase any sort of attractor flies.

A few years later I asked our shop's guides to keep records of stomach samples from the steelhead for each month of the season. The feeding pattern was very clear. In the fall, the samples included mainly green rock worms (caddis larvae) and salmon eggs. In January and February, they were almost entirely tiny black winter stoneflies, which emerge from the stream on sunny afternoons. During the spring spawning run, the fish fed on steelhead and sucker eggs and larger black stoneflies.

We were surprised not to find wigglers (*Hexagenia* nymphs), which were the fly of choice of anglers. We later learned that those nymphs migrated mainly during high water when there were few fishermen out. Surprisingly, there was only one minnow in the season's sampling, which indicated that the steelhead fed like trout, feeding on drifting nymphs rather than chasing minnows. From our samplings, we learned that you could readily catch steelhead if you gave them the right options in season.

Some steelhead run into the rivers in the fall but the number varies. I sometimes call it the mythical fall steelhead run. Some years, there are few. Other years, the run is heavy.

* * * * *

I was walking near the Pere Marquette River one fall when the steelhead run was heavy. A fisherman who was a customer of mine approached me and said, "Dick, this run is so great. I was supposed to be home three days ago—would you call my wife and tell her I will be a few more days?" That went beyond the bounds of good customer service, and I told him to call his own wife.

* * * * *

The main steelhead spawning run is in late March and April in Michigan rivers. While the fish do not feed heavily at that time, they do still eat, picking up drifting eggs and nymphs.

I learned a hard lesson one spring day, when I drove my car on a snowy road to get closer to the river. The snow was frozen when I drove down the road that morning, but later in the day the sun had softened the snow and I found myself hopelessly stuck. Even a wrecker could not pull me out. That car sat in the woods for nearly a month before the snow melted enough to drive out.

Mike Fong, a West Coast steelhead angler, visited us that spring. When we arrived at Barothy Lodge on the Pere Marquette River, we asked the returning anglers how they did. One said he caught five fish, another eight, and another three. Mike was amazed at the large number of fish in the run. He said he had never caught three steelhead in one day in his life.

Salmon

The introduction of Pacific salmon into the Great Lakes in the early

Steelhead on the Pere Marquette.

1970s was a monumental event in sportfishing, and most anglers were very excited. Around that time, I was transferred to Toledo, Ohio. I had long admired Buck Juhasz, a shop owner from Cleveland, so I called to see if we could get together to fish for salmon. "Sure thing," he said. "I'll meet you in Milan, in the parking lot under the bridge that crosses the Huron River in the center of town, at noon this Sunday."

I went to Milan, found the bridge over the Huron River, parked in the lot under the bridge, and waited . . . and waited . . . and waited. No Buck.

Monday morning I called and asked him where he had been. "I was right there," he said.

"Where were you?" I replied. "I was right there, and waited for three hours."

We finally figured it out. I had been in Milan, Michigan, under the bridge over Michigan's Huron River, and Buck had been in Milan, Ohio, under the bridge on Ohio's Huron River.

■ ■ ■ ■ ■

Pacific salmon and steelhead are two different stories. Since salmon do not eat during the spawning run, it is not so easy to get them to take a fly. Many anglers have found that if you swing a streamer by a salmon, it might take the fly or be "lined," or hooked by the line running through its mouth. You could also snag a fin by swinging a streamer. I learned to stand downstream from the salmon, cast the fly upstream above the fish, and let it dead-drift to or past them. If a fish does not take, the fly simply drifts by without snagging, and you cast again.

After several days in the river, the average salmon is neither very strong nor very aggressive. But a large male fresh out of the lake is a tough fish to land because you have little room to play it in a river. In general, if the fish jumps clear of the water five or six times, you will not land it. It will break free from your line.

* * * * *

Because salmon can be tough to catch, Michigan's natural resources department decided to promote snagging sometime in the 1980s. The method involved jerking a treble hook weighted with lead through the water until it snagged a fish. There was no sport or skill involved. The department sent people out to lecture to sports groups, recommending this practice. As a result, the streams were soon loaded with people snagging and killing up to five fish a day. Litter and personal confrontations became common.

I was the fisheries coordinator for Michigan Trout Unlimited at the time. TU led the way by starting an anti-snagging coalition that also included the Federation of Fly Fishers and the Michigan Guides' Association. We found opposition from Michigan United Conservation Clubs (MUCC) and the Michigan Salmon and Steelhead Fishermen's Association. This meant that every time we made a presentation to a government agency, they were there opposing us. It was embarrassing and counterproductive.

We decided to try to change the policies of MUCC. The organization's president, Tom Washington, said the club chapters favored snagging because most of their members were hunters who only fished occasionally. It was easier to snag the fish than take them with lures or flies. We suggested that MUCC should not stand in opposition to all the other fishing groups in the state, as that would force us to take the position that the clubs did not represent fishermen. Tom Washington agreed, and the MUCC policy was changed.

The Salmon and Steelhead Fishermen's Association said their members were mainly interested in fishing in the Great Lakes. We offered to support their lake proposals if they would support our river proposals. We then traveled around explaining this to their members and ended up with unanimity among the fishing organizations, forming a Sportfishing Coalition.

After a few years we got snagging eliminated, at least legally. All sportsmen know eternal vigilance and action is essential to protecting our sport.

Tribal Fishing

In one case, the federal government helped our conservation efforts. A good friend of mine was appointed federal district judge. His predecessor had ruled that the American Indian tribes were free of all government rules and the tribes had been taking the position they were not subject to the conservation laws. I won't quote the judge's words, but his ruling was to the effect that the tribes had to live responsibly with the rest of the nation. He then appointed a mediator for the court. If the parties could not work things out, the judge ruled that he himself would decide what the rules were. The parties did finally reach agreement. There were some compromises, but it has helped maintain a reasonable relationship.

Winter Guiding

When we were guiding clients for winter steelhead fishing, we had to be careful they didn't get too wet or cold, or lost. Three young men from Chicago wanted to be guided to some fishing but our guides were fully booked. So I was elected.

We were to fish the Pere Marquette, which meanders a lot. It is common for a river to have two miles of stream for one mile of road, but much of the Pere Marquette has four miles of river for one mile of road. Plus, a lot of it is in wooded and brushy country. It is easy to get lost and think you are going the right way.

When we got to the river I asked my clients if they had compasses. None of them did.

No problem. I explained to the young Chicagoans that if you point the hour hand of your watch at the sun and then find the point halfway between the hour hand and twelve o'clock, that will be south. (Caution: Do not rely on this in the Southern Hemisphere, or at night.) All three looked at their watches—they were digital. "So much for that," I said. "Just stay with me."

20 FISHING WITH JAKE

My grandson, Jake, has been a regular fishing companion since the age of four. For several years now he can be counted on to spot the onset of a new hatch even before I do. This is especially helpful since the flies are getting a bit too small for me to see. It's amazing how they shrink.

Jake liked to go with me on fishing trips from his earliest years. I would place him in the bow seat of my canoe and let him swing a wet fly wherever he wanted, while I waded and maneuvered the canoe to put him in good spots. He caught a few fish that way. If he preferred to catch frogs, I would beach the canoe and let him do that. He was once asked where he liked to fish with me. He answered, "Anywhere!"

One day we stopped for a Coke. I sat Jake on a barstool and patted him on the shoulder, telling him I was glad he came with me. He said, "Do dat again." I asked if he meant the pat or what I said. His reply was "Bofe."

Their Mommy Won't Let 'Em

On our way to the stream one day, Jake spotted a beat-up junker of a truck with a couple of grungy men in the cab.

"Pop Pop, what's wrong with that truck?" he asked.

"It needs to be painted," I replied

"Yeah," he said thoughtfully, "and their mommy won't let 'em."

I asked his mother what prompted that reply, and was advised he had recently attempted to redecorate their favorite sofa with permanent markers. Obviously, his mommy wouldn't let him.

■ ■ ■ ■ ■

In my den one day, Jake saw a print of a brook trout jumping from the water, about to snatch a mayfly from the air. "Pop Pop," he asked, "is that fish going to eat that fly?" "Yes," I answered, to which Jake replied, "He's going to get sick!"

Not the Bad Carrots

When Jake was four, I was asked to give a talk to the Chicago Angler's Club and thought it would be a good time for him to go on his first train ride. Upon boarding, I walked him through the cars he was allowed to go into and then gave him his rein as I sat in my coach seat. As I had expected he was soon scouting the other cars.

Jake found out the car ahead of ours was a smoking car, and he walked the length of it waving away smoke and telling the riders they should not smoke. The car beyond, he reported, smelled like carrots—"not the bad carrots, the good ones." He even convinced a young schoolgirl across the aisle to go with him to smell the carrots.

When we got to Chicago, I took him to the observation deck of the Hancock Building, one of the city's tallest, with a beautiful view of downtown and the lakefront. We then headed to the meeting place of the Angler's Club. Jake seemed intimidated by the roomful of older suited men, but he relaxed when they served the food. When they started to applaud my remarks and seem friendly, he relaxed a bit more and decided they were all right.

When my talk was over and it was time to leave, I stood by the door to shake hands. Jake stood next to me and did what four-year-olds do—he gave each man a hug. The men chuckled and invited Jake to come back.

JAKE AND DICK POBST

"Do you have much experience teaching people?"—Jake

156

Do You Have Much Experience?

When Jake was six, I was still just letting him swing a wet fly. By then he was wading, but I had not yet taught him anything about fishing a dry fly during a hatch.

One evening we found ourselves in the middle of a good sulphur hatch. I tied a dry fly on his leader, then decided to teach him what I could. My instructions were fast and furious: "Let the fly drift!" "Set the hook!" "Keep the line tight!" "Now let him run!" "Keep a bend in the rod!" "Now reel in!" "Let him drift into my net!" You get the idea. He caught three trout on dry flies that evening, and could not have been happier. He bubbled all the way to the car.

On the drive home, however, he grew quiet. After a while he asked, "Pop Pop, do you have much experience teaching people?" The next day I enrolled him in one of our shop's fishing schools and told him we would fish again when he completed the course.

The Lemonade Stand

The first day of fishing school we always asked our students to introduce themselves and state their professions, what fishing experience they have, and what sort of fishing they expect to do. During Jake's session, we went through a psychiatrist, a teacher, a lawyer, and a store owner before coming to him. Jake said, "I run a lemonade stand." That got a good laugh from the adults.

Here's the rest of the story. Business was slow at the lemonade stand, so Jake and his partner rode their bikes to a playground to solicit business. The clients had to pay up front at the playground before they went down the block to the stand to get their lemonade. The first group attracted others, and soon there was a large, racially mixed gang at the stand. The police came to investigate, and Jake and his partner insisted the cops buy lemonade. The boys made $17 that day. They learned how to sell and to handle a mixed crowd. Not a bad lesson.

■ ■ ■ ■ ■

Hunting and fishing are part of the ethos in the North Woods. When our daughter, a teacher, asked a young boy from the country to name the four seasons, he answered, "Well, there's trout season, salmon season, deer season, and rabbit season."

Maybe he learned the seasons at Joe's Day Care.

KIDS LEARN THE SEASONS AT JOE'S.

PART IV: Trout Stream Insects, 1985–2011

21 *TROUT STREAM INSECTS* & OTHER WORKS

Super Hatches Video

My interest in fly hatches had a shaky start after Nancy and I founded our fly shop. Carl Richards, coauthor of *Selective Trout*, and I made a videotape called *Super Hatches* with videographer Steve Spengler. We thought that the use of live color pictures was a good way to explain fly hatches, and the video provided a simple and clear way to learn the flies.

Most critics were very complimentary. Nelson Bryant of the *New York Times* said it was "superb." A good friend came into our shop waving a copy of Bryant's article, exclaiming, "They called it superb! The *Times* never called anything superb!"

One major critic demurred. He said Carl and I could not act (true, but our price was right) and, anyway, the videotape should have been a book. I honestly did not understand. Shouldn't it be criticized as a video? Should the Bible have been a movie? I complained to the editor.

The tape sold reasonably well as fly-fishing tapes go but it wouldn't pay the rent.

Don Jones, a fly shop operator from Lake Placid, approached me one day and said he loved the tape and used it in all his fishing classes. "But I always apologize for it," he added. When I asked him why, Don replied, "I always tell the students that Carl and Dick are just laid-back Midwesterners. It takes them all day to say anything. But when they get done it is really worthwhile."

Trout Stream Insects

Perk Perkins, who was by that time president of Orvis, asked me in 1989 if I could adapt the simple pictorial method used in the *Super Hatches* video to write a pocketsize book about the hatches. As I worked on the project, it finally dawned on me that the critic had been right all along. Such a book could be used as a reference source, whereas it was not practical to use a video that way.

The book would need to cover America's major hatches separated into Eastern and Western sections. It would also need to include color pictures of each stage of the insects, with each hatch covered on one page, shown in the order of hatching. The common name or names would be prominent, but the Latin names would be included as well. The size of the fly, the hook size, and possible patterns would be included. In addition, the life cycles and the hatch charts—East and West—would be shown. It would include mayflies, caddisflies, stoneflies, midges, and terrestrials.

I put a draft together about the size of a deck of playing cards and under a quarter inch thick. I then sent it to Nick Lyons, who printed books for Orvis, and he sent it right back, saying it was too short and too small to display on a bookcase. The problem had been that in making it small, I just left out some information. It was easy to make it bigger.

A number of chapters were added, such as "How to Use This Book," "What Trout Eat," "The Four Main Trout Stream Insects," "Eastern and Western Hatch Charts," "The Life Cycle of the Mayfly," and so forth. We named it *Trout Stream Insects*, and Nick published it in 1991. Using the hatch chart anglers can select artificial flies similar to those that are supposed to hatch, and go to the river prepared with the most likely choices. Oh, yes, it also fits in your pocket.

To avoid having to use microscopes and entomological keys, I added simple clues visible to the naked eye, such as wing markings, number of tails, hook size, body color, and time of year.

The book has been through seventeen printings and has now been revised and reissued. I had to eat a lot of crow for not understanding the critic and for complaining about him. *Trout Stream Insects* has sold over ninety thousand copies—not one of the blockbusters, but a solid book for the small fly-fishing industry, nevertheless.

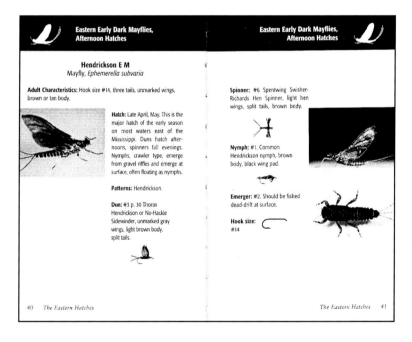

SAMPLE PAGES FROM *TROUT STREAM INSECTS*.

■ ■ ■ ■ ■

A frequent question I hear is "How do you pronounce the Latin names of insects?" The answer is that Latin is a dead language and no one in recent centuries has heard it pronounced by a native speaker of Latin. If you asked a Latin teacher, a priest, and an entomologist to pronounce a name, they would seldom agree. So just pronounce it like you would pronounce items on a menu in an Italian restaurant. Ask the waiter if necessary.

The Caddisfly Handbook

Several years after *Trout Stream Insects* was published Carl Richards asked me what I thought was the most important subject for a book on practical entomology that had not yet been done. I suggested caddisflies. No one had ever used a "super hatches" approach to caddis, and it was vitally needed. This means you focus on the hatches that are of major importance and ignore the rest. Many books and scientific works list every possible insect but few of us will ever see the great majority of them.

At the time, caddis fishing was far too complicated. The authoritative book was *Caddisflies* by Gary LaFontaine. It listed 193 species of caddis, and we had no way of figuring out which were important— damned few as it turned out.

Carl and I started our work on caddisflies in the mid-1990s. Carl caught and analyzed the insects around the clock, often camping out several nights a week to understand what was happening. Most of our caddis fishing was done on the Muskegon River, which had great hatches but was tough to fish. We found that in our tailwater on the Muskegon there were two caddisflies in significant quantities, both of the family *Hydropsychidae*. This made figuring out their behavior much simpler.

Carl's work on the practical entomology of caddisflies led to our cowriting *The Caddisfly Handbook*. As a research project, it was one of his best. My function was to check out the Rocky Mountain hatches.

That was very nice duty. John Juracek of Blue Ribbon Fly Shop and author Dave Hughes helped me immensely in checking out our facts.

The Vest Pocket Guides

Fifteen years after the publication of *Trout Stream Insects*, the Lyons Press decided to revise and update both it and *The Caddisfly Handbook* in paperback. They have been made into separate, smaller books titled *The Orvis Vest Pocket Guide to Mayflies* and *The Orvis Vest Pocket Guide to Caddisflies*. In addition to updated information the books contain new digital photos. They are handier to carry and use in the field than their predecessors.

■ ■ ■ ■

I always concentrated on simple ways of understanding the insects, and did not delve into the entomology the way Carl did. Nevertheless, I am often introduced as an entomologist. I ask the audience if they remember Nixon's saying, "I am not a crook." Well, I am not an entomologist, just a practical fisherman.

SILENT KNIGHT

On slow days they build armor at the body shop. Maybe they'd be busier if we could read their sign.

22 MOTHER'S DAY & OTHER DAYS

Mother's Day was the day I took the kids out so Mom got some peace and quiet, so I never fished on that day.

But I always loved to fish in the spring. One of our early hatches in the East is the little black caddis. In the West a closely related caddisfly is known as the Mother's Day caddis. It occurs in the spring before snowmelt on the mountains. At lower elevations it is a great time to be around Yellowstone National Park. The grass is greening up in the valley and the wild animals start to congregate there. You can see buffalo, elk, deer, antelope, mountain goats, sheep, and eagles, to mention a few.

While fishing on the spring creeks of Paradise Valley at the end of April a few years ago the guide and I encountered the Mother's Day hatch and had some great fishing. This was in the Yellowstone valley just upstream from Livingston between the Absaroka and Gallatin Ranges. When I asked the guide how the hatch got its name, he said it actually started before Mother's Day, but the guides named it the Mother's Day hatch so they could get in some fishing before they got so busy guiding that they couldn't fish.

You can imagine my delight when I spotted this sign outside a convenience store:

ON THE WAY TO FISH THE MOTHER'S DAY
CADDIS HATCH. NO DOUBT MOM IS WAITING
FOR THE BEER AND WORMS.

But look at the simple rule for the use of the apostrophe: Don't worry if it is singular, plural, or possessive—just stick it on after the *s*.

The Brown Palace

When in Colorado, Nancy and I would stop over at the Brown Palace Hotel in Denver whenever possible. It is a charming old hotel with a history and a present. The present includes excellent cuisine and a great atmosphere. The history includes an underground passageway to what used to be a brothel but is now a museum of western art, including numerous works of artists Frederic Remington and Charlie Russell. The hotel is named for the family of Molly Brown, famous for her heroism and survival of the Titanic disaster. She was portrayed by Debbie Reynolds in the Movie *The Unsinkable Molly Brown*.

If you visit the hotel, notice the grand staircase that leads into the lobby. That is where Denver society used to present its debutantes and auction its prize bulls—Denver's breeding stock, as someone explained it.

A Treat for the Lady

I seldom use a canoe to fish, choosing either to wade or use a drift boat in large rivers. However, one day I needed a canoe to reach a couple of spots some distance away on the Michigan Platte. This river is noted for tight bends and overly brushy banks. It is frequented by recreational canoeists who are often noted for their poor canoe technique.

A middle-aged couple launched ahead of me. I thought how nice it was of him to take his lady canoeing on a beautiful trout stream on a beautiful day. It was an inappropriate thought. They were not around the first bend before the lady, seated in the bow with zero canoeing skill, started cussing out the man. He at least understood that the stern paddler was responsible for maneuvering the canoe although he knew little about how to do it. I could hear the woman's raucous voice as they preceded me down the stream. She had many opinions about what the steersman was doing wrong.

It was not long before they approached a tight ninety-degree bend in the river. The bank ahead was covered with branches leaning halfway across the stream. Their canoe went bow-first into the bushes, which forced the woman to the bottom of the canoe on her back. She could do nothing, and the level and volume of her invective tripled: "You dumb @#%&*—get me out of here!"

The man carefully stepped out of the canoe, said "Like hell!" and walked away, leaving her on her back in the bottom of the canoe. I was able to pull the canoe out of the bushes, sympathetic to the guy's feelings, but as the song says, "That Ain't No Way to Treat a Lady." I'll bet he forgot Mother's Day and Ladies' Day, too.

Wisconsin's Spring Creeks

I drove to the fabled spring creeks of southwestern Wisconsin to fish with friends there. I can't remember the names of all the streams I fished, but they are high-quality spring creeks. Black Earth Creek is one, but my favorites were Castle Rock and Timber Coulee.

Much of the water runs through pastures for dairy cattle. In the years I fished there the cattle roamed freely through the streams. A couple of us thought we should buy those white waders made for some industrial uses and paint big black spots on them so the fish would think we were Holsteins. It was another good idea that never materialized. I think the market was too small.

Like most spring creeks the water is clear and the fish are not easy to deceive. There are good hatches, and you can find good local guides who know the rivers and the accesses. It is well worth spending some time fishing there.

* * * * *

It is a long drive from my home in Michigan to the spring creeks of southwestern Wisconsin, and I often passed the time listening to the radio. One morning, Michael Feldman, the radio talk show host, was holding a mock contest to find a new slogan for Wisconsin's license plates. He thought "America's Dairyland" was sort of quaint.

Wisconsinites have a love/hate relationship with the Chicagoans who come up to fish their streams. They love their money but hate their traffic. Many suggestions were considered, but the winner, hands down, was "Come Up and Smell Our Dairy Air."

∗ ∗ ∗ ∗ ∗

Another way to pass the time on long trips is to sing. I sing the old popular songs and play the guitar as a hobby, and singing while I drive gives me practice and helps me remember the words. To begin a song it is vital to remember the first line. Even if I know the title, I am lost without the first line. One morning I had a song in mind but could not think of the words to save myself. It was a long time before I got it. The first line was "You must remember this . . ."

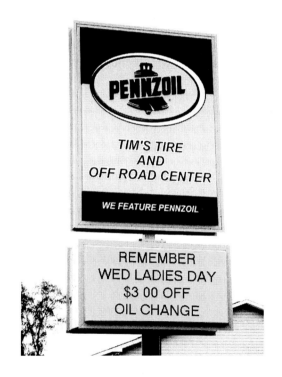

IT IS WELL KNOWN LADIES LOVE OIL.

23 JOHN VOELKER'S *TESTAMENT*

I made the *Super Hatches* video with Carl Richards in the mid-1980s under the trade name Thornapple Angling Classics. Sometime in 1986 Nick Lyons called. He asked why I used that trade name. I told him I intended to produce "how-to" videos and some of historical interest. He then asked if I would be interested in producing a video showing some original movie footage by John Voelker. Without any hesitation, the answer was an emphatic "Yes!"

Nick explained that he had talked to Elihu Winer, who had written the stage play adaptation of *Anatomy of a Murder*, which had been performed successfully in New York. In the process, Winer had become interested in Voelker. He hired a cinematographer and went to Michigan's UP to film John fishing in his native habitat. This was intended to be a short subject for the movies, but shorts had fallen out of fashion before the film could be used. John had written *Testament of a Fisherman*, later famous among anglers, to be used as a theme for the movie.

We made the film into a video called *Trout Madness* around 1987. I lost money on it, but I'd do it again in a heartbeat. It showed John in his native habitat, fishing on his favorite streams and ponds as he always did. John always referred to the video as "*Testament.*"

■ ■ ■ ■ ■

When John was well into his eighties, he phoned to say he needed a small boat that he could load onto his "fish car" and use to get into hidden trout ponds too far away to walk to. I suggested a Kentucky poke boat and told him where to get one, but I'm not aware he ever did. The fact that a man in his eighties would even think about such an undertaking epitomized John's ardor for fishing.

■ ■ ■ ■ ■

Knowing John was getting frail, I was eager to have him see my latest book, *Trout Stream Insects*, and rushed it to the post office as soon as I got it. A few days later I read he had died, and I despaired of his having seen the book.

The day John died, he wrote me a letter, which his widow, Grace, sent me. The letter read:

> Ishpeming
> March 18, 1991
>
> Dear Dick,
>   Thank you for your letter and for your handsome new book with the generous inscription.
>   Writing's like fishing—there's a lot of luck in both.
>   But I thank you for liking "Testament" and giving it a try.
>
> Good luck and warm regards. John

That was generous, as John thought people who wrote books about fly hatches took all the skill and mystery out of fishing and made it too easy. Furthermore, he did not want to be bothered read-ing everybody's crazy theories and fantasies, and he said uncharitable things about "scientific anglers." I wish I could have informed him that the odds are still in favor of the trout. I have been skunked more than once since writing the book. An interesting thing about John was that he could make fun of my theories in such a good-humored way that I remained fond of him.

＊ ＊ ＊ ＊ ＊

The following was written as the theme for the video *Trout Madness*:

TESTAMENT OF A FISHERMAN

I fish because I love to; because I love the environs where trout are found, which are invariably beautiful, and hate the environs where crowds of people are found, which are invariably ugly; because of all the television commercials, cocktail parties, and assorted social posturing I thus escape; because in a world where most men seem to spend their lives doing things they hate, my fishing is at once an endless source of delight and an act of small rebellion; because trout do not lie or cheat and cannot be bought or bribed or impressed by power, but respond only to quietude and humility and endless patience; because I suspect that men are going along this way for the last time, and I don't want to waste the trip; because mercifully there are no telephones on trout waters; because only in the woods can I find solitude without loneliness; because bourbon out of an old tin cup always tastes better out there; because maybe one day I will catch a mermaid; and, finally, not because I regard fishing as being so terribly important but because I suspect that so many of the other concerns of men are equally unimportant—and not nearly so much fun.

John Voelker
(Robert Traver)

ENTERING THE RESERVATION—ILL EAGLE?

OH, ILLEGAL—WHAT ARE YOU GOING
TO DO ABOUT IT, PALEFACE?

24 I'M GOING TO CRY—THE ROCKIES

Around 2008 John Miller, the photographer/entomologist who did the photos for *The Orvis Pocket Guide to Mayflies*, invited me to fish the West Branch of the Delaware in New York. While there, we spent a great day fishing with Al Caucci, coauthor of the classic book *Hatches II*. The only downside to the day was launching from the sewage treatment plant. I thought Al Caucci's home launch should have a more dignified title.

Al asked me why the midwestern writers wrote so little about eastern fly fishing. I thought this was due to a couple of things: First, the eastern writers had thoroughly covered that subject. Second, there were more new hatches to learn about in the Rockies.

By the 1980s there were a lot of very good fly shops, writers, and guides in the Rockies from whom we were learning a lot. Not only did the Rockies have mayfly hatches that were new to us, but midges, stoneflies, and caddisflies were generally more important there.

Hatch Classes

Mark Bressler of Orvis asked me to conduct annual fly hatch classes for the Rocky Mountain guides. These classes took place throughout the 1990s. I would take a few days to scout out the area where the meetings were held. I would then show slides of the local aquatic insects to the group before taking them to a river or two to show how to put the knowledge in action.

For example, we would go to a spring creek for a demonstration on how to hold a screen in the surface to see what kind of fly shucks were floating down and identify the insects. We would then move upstream until we found rising fish and discover how you could catch those fish by imitating the flies we had found downstream. Seining nymphs from the river bottom can tell you what will hatch later, but checking floating shucks tells you what is happening upstream now.

Some years the hatch classes took place in Jackson Hole, other times in West Yellowstone or Glendale, Colorado, and for a few years they took place in Cody, Wyoming.

        ■ ■ ■ ■ ■

I learned as much as I taught on those trips. Once I was fishing with my host on the White River near Meeker, Colorado, and mentioned that I had never been able to figure out nymphing with a strike indicator. He took me to one of the tributaries, and we rigged one rod with a strike indicator and nymph. He said we were playing baseball. One of us would take the rod and fish until he missed three strikes, then it went to the other one. If you wanted to catch fish you had to pay attention to all the details.

I understood indicator nymph fishing and complex line mending (essential to getting a natural drift of the nymph) pretty well by the end of the afternoon. This is a phase of hatch matching. Before swimming to the surface to hatch the nymphs of many flies drift along the bottom. Pre-emergence drift can give you an extra hour or more of good fishing before the duns pop. Just fish the weighted nymph of the expected hatch along the bottom, then as a floating nymph when the first fish rise, before they take duns. Some people think fish always feed on nymphs but not nearly as much as during pre-emergence drift.

GOOD POINT!

They finally fixed the road that runs north out of Meeker.

The Green Drake Hatch

The western green drake hatch is as exciting a hatch to fish as any I know. They hatch in the middle of the day and the biggest fish around will rise to the duns.

Once while fishing Elk Creek in Colorado with favorite guide Ted Relihan, a green drake hatch gave us spectacular fishing for an hour or more. My record catch on that hatch was calculated at seven pounds using the measurement method: Length times girth (squared) divided by 800 equals weight in pounds. This was on a stream not more than twenty feet wide.

The night before a hellish thunderstorm had rolled down the narrow mountain valley, sending all the anglers racing for their trucks. Next morning, nothing was rising. We assumed the storm had satiated the fish with worms—we were not getting a touch.

Ted prodded me by saying he thought I knew how to fish. "Oh, so you want me to catch fish?" I snorted. "Hold my fly rod for a minute, and after I relieve myself in the bushes, I will start catching fish!"

The moment I took my rod back the drakes started to pop and every fish in the stream was taking them. Idle boasts are sometimes worth a try. I felt sort of like Ali stating he would "whup" Liston, but with less justification.

After an hour Ted informed me I had just completed a Rocky Mountain grand slam: rainbow, cutthroat, cuttbow, brown, and brookie. I opted to quit fishing and go have lunch. It would be gilding the lily to fish any more that day.

The memory of the grand slam is one good reason Ted is a favorite guide and fishing companion.

■ ■ ■ ■ ■

While fishing with Ted I decided I should take more pictures on my trips—scenery, flowers, something besides fish and fishermen. I had the idea this would make my lectures a little more palatable to some of the gals in my classes. There were quite a few wildflowers in bloom, so I took pictures of several of them.

After I had the photos developed I realized I had no idea what kind of flowers they were. I sent prints to Ted and asked him to write the names of the flowers on the back of the prints and return them to me. He wrote: "Little white flower." "Little blue flower." "Little red flower."

That was the end of my taking flower pictures. I went back to photographing fish, fishermen, and signs.

I'm Going to Cry!

On another trip to Colorado, our host arranged for a float trip on Utah's Green River below Flaming Gorge Reservoir. We flew over from Meeker, Colorado, in a couple of small planes piloted by a father and son who were forest fire spotters in season.

My grandson had told me he'd like to be a fire spotter so I quizzed the pilots about the life. The father said it sometimes got tiresome when there were no fires. A couple of times while flying alone, he had even fallen asleep from boredom. "But one year was just great!" he exclaimed. "That was fun! I spotted seventy-eight fires that year." I guess it might be considered fun provided you were up in an airplane.

We arrived at our starting point outside the town of Dutch John, adjacent to the Flaming Gorge Dam, and found a half-dozen guides waiting with their drift boats. While we unpacked our gear, they talked the usual macho BS about who caught the most or biggest fish and who had the most to drink the night before.

The wind was so strong the guides had to wait for lulls to row downstream and around the bends. Meanwhile, I suggested we move to the lee of the bank and fish the calm waters there. As soon as we did, we saw rising fish. I thought they were midging and put on a floating pupa. Sure enough, in short order I caught three decent fish, watching them rise several feet in the clear water to take the fly. There is nothing more exciting in fishing than watching that slow rise to the fly.

The guide turned to my partner and said, "Tony, let me have your rod and I'll rig it like Dick's." I handed Tony my rod, and told him to catch something while he waited. "What?!" exclaimed the guide. "You are going to let him use your rod? I never heard of anything as nice

THESE GUYS DID NOT BUILD OUR DRIFT BOAT.

as that. I think I'm going to cry!" All this bleated by one of the macho guides.

Regarding those midges, I have read that 90 percent of midges taken at the surface are floating pupae, which is worth knowing. An imitation of the floating pupa is far and away the most likely fly to catch fish during a midge emergence. I called Tom Travis, a friend and guide from Livingston, and asked his opinion. Tom agreed about the emergence, but pointed out that when there are mating clusters, you need a Griffith's Gnat. To round out the picture, San Juan worms are midge larvae, a required fly pattern before emergence.

We eventually made our way downstream and came upon a typical mountain cabin, next to a big waterwheel. The guide told me that before the gorge was dammed Butch Cassidy and the Sundance Kid used the cabin as a hideout. They would carry out a season of robberies and then ride to the top of the gorge, where they had stashed a raft. They would then take the raft through the gorge, leaving pursuers and their horses behind, and winter in the cabin.

Brokaw's Cabin

While we are on the subject of cabins, there is a modern tale to tell. One of our Michigan outdoors painters, and a very good friend and fisherman, Bud Kanouse, brought some paintings into our shop to sell. One was of a western streamside cabin titled *Brokaw's Cabin*.

The painting had not sold by Christmas, which is the prime time for selling paintings, so Nancy sent a picture of it to Tom Brokaw. He immediately sent us a check with a note asking us to send it to him—however, he wrote, it was not his cabin.

Nancy contacted Bud, who checked and found out the cabin belonged to Charles Kuralt and its ownership was disputed in his palimony suit. So "Brokaw's Cabin" had a double life in palimony and a Wild West life of its own.

The Big Blackfoot

Late one night I drove to Montana outfitter Paul Roos's tent camp on the Big Blackfoot, the river featured in the book *A River Runs Through It*. There were directions to my tent on the gate, so I found it and tumbled into the sack. The next morning I got up glorying in the sunshine and the joy of being in the wilderness. I went to the mess tent and got a cup of coffee, then went outside to take a look around.

In my wilderness paradise, across the river, was a ranch raising emus, of all ridiculous things. I had been dreaming of longhorn cattle or wild mustangs, not emus from Australia. It was sort of a letdown but the fishing made up for it.

It pleased me to know I was treading some of the same ground as Lewis and Clark as they descended from the Continental Divide to the Pacific. I had brought a copy of Steven Ambrose's book *Undaunted Courage* along and reread it in the evenings. It made me feel right at home on the trail of the great explorers.

■ ■ ■ ■ ■

This trip was in early August. After a few days' fishing I went into Lincoln for dinner, then started driving south after dark. Around midnight I ran into whiteout conditions in MacDonald Pass and ended up sleeping a couple of hours in the car until the snow stopped. I then headed on down to Sheridan, Montana, where the Kanouses had invited me to stay and fish.

By the time I got to Sheridan, it was getting close to dinnertime. I thought I should take my hosts a bottle of wine, so I stopped in the only grocery store and perused the wine selection. I had a choice between Ripple and Mogen David—a good lesson in not leaving shopping until the last moment. I had to drive several more miles to get a more or less acceptable bottle of wine, which was labeled "Red Table Wine." It lived up to its label but without a lot to spare.

20 Percent Lighter

I ran into an old friend in Denver, a well-known fly-fishing writer who will remain nameless. When I asked him what he was doing, he said he had just quit his job and was going to do freelance writing, mainly for the magazines, and maybe a book. I said, "Great, you'll

$400

CASH

REWARD

And two cases of free beer

  For information that leads to the retrieval of the two stolen *HP* laptops computer's from bunkhouse (08/22/08) room # 201 belonging to Willie H. & Valentine T.
  This information will be kept anonymous except to law enforcement officials.

Thank you for your attention and interest in this matter.

Willie & Valentine
(visit us at bunk house)

NOT YOUR FATHER'S BUNKHOUSE.

be good at that! But do me one favor. Don't write anything about fly rods that are now '20 percent lighter and 30 percent stronger' or '30 percent lighter and 20 percent stronger.' For the past ten years, that has been done ad nauseam, and it is ridiculous! At that rate, rods would be levitating by now."

His face lost all expression after that comment. Within a week I found a magazine in which an article of his appeared. It claimed the latest rod was "20 percent lighter and 30 percent stronger." I don't know which of us was more embarrassed by that—I suspect we were about even. I hope time will make it humorous.

Once more, I may have to eat crow. I just fell in love with, and bought, one of Orvis's latest fly rods, the Helios ZG. It is light and has a smooth, crisp action. And I'll be darned if it isn't either 30 percent lighter and 20 percent stronger, or the reverse. The important part, though, is that it casts better than any other rod I ever held. So if it levitates on opening day, crow will be on the menu.

Crow is not bad once you acquire the taste. It does not, however, taste like chicken.

LINCOLN LOGS

Between Cody, Wyoming, and Fort Smith, Montana, in case
you need logs.

25 YOU MIGHT MATCH THE HATCH, BUT YOU COULDN'T MATCH ERNIE

Ernie Schwiebert was not often funny but he was always amazing. He published his classic *Matching the Hatch* while still in college. He had actually written it when he was in his middle teens while living in Europe but couldn't find a publisher. When he returned to college in the United States, he rewrote the book according to U.S. entomology. Ernie's wealth of knowledge is evident in his two-volume encyclopedia *Trout*, which covered just about everything related to trout fishing.

I have never met a more widely traveled fisherman. Ernie caught his first trout on a dry fly—a light cahill—on Michigan's Pere Marquette River at the age of five. By the time he was thirty, he had fished all over the United States, Canada, Europe, and South America. He studied and remembered just about everything he ever encountered. One of the most intriguing things about Ernie was his endless supply of stories. He could talk for hours about his early days fishing in Michigan and the American West. He was also active in just about every organization remotely related to fly fishing.

When Ernie was asked whether you needed to know all about the hatches to fish he said, "It depends on how good you want to be. The streams are more complicated than people know, and if you want to do well you need to study the cycles and habitat. A good fisherman will wait until the conditions are right. For example, the hendricksons will hatch just about 2:30—sun time, not daylight saving time—and he will get ready to fish at about that time."

Carl Richards introduced me to Ernie, and the three of us had many great days fishing Ernie's old Michigan haunts. Many people found Ernie contentious—he was often involved in arguments and he didn't lose a lot. Carl and I realized Ernie had special talents and we felt there was no point trying to beat him at his game. He had a wealth of knowledge, and we liked to get him to display it.

Hendrickson Time

In the early 1990s, Ernie and I decided to make a video called *Hendrickson Time* featuring Ernie. It was situated on Michigan's Au Sable River, and we operated out of the old lodge of the great rod maker Paul Young. I was the logistics guy and scriptwriter. Steve Spengler, who had taped the *Super Hatches* video, was the videographer. *Hendrickson Time* was never published because the studio that retained some rights went broke, and a release could not be obtained.

Amazingly, Ernie did not need a script. He would ask what was next on the shooting outline, and I would say something like "Tell us how the fly got its name—hendrickson." Ernie would pause and then deliver a flawless lecture on the origin of the name. When I asked about the Latin name, he talked not only about the hendrickson, *Ephemerella subvaria*, but also about a half-dozen other flies that occur around the same time.

When I asked him to tell us about the Au Sable, he gave a lecture on the history of the river, the early settlers, and the effects of the logging industry, adding, "We're in what some people call the Whip-poorwill stretch, with Black Bend below and Stephan Bridge above. It's a zone of the river that doubles its volume without a tributary. The reason is an endless cycle of limestone springs full of watercress in the summer, which means that this stretch of the river system is one of the earliest and pretty reliable for the early fly hatches."

Further on he said, "A nice thing about trout this time of the year is that the trout are pretty much civilized. They don't get up until late in the morning, and unless there is a spinner fall about twilight, the fishing is pretty much over by the time people go in for adult beverages, late in the afternoon." Ernie was a spellbinding speaker.

While we were taping, Ernie announced that he would tie a fly at streamside without a vise. He had a small packet that contained hackle pliers, scissors, some hooks, thread, and tying materials. Using the hackle pliers as a bobbin, he wound thread on the hook, whip-finished it, and then held the hook in his lips while he prepared his materials. His first fly was to be a gold-ribbed hare's ear, and the gold rib was "a piece of wire from a bottle of Grand Macnish, which made collecting the materials more fun than tying the fly." He then demonstrated another use for a wedding veil, besides nymph netting, by tying a hendrickson spinner with a piece of veil as wings.

* * * * *

Ernie and I were invited to spend a few days at Nash Camp, on the North Branch of the Au Sable, while we were taping *Hendrickson Time*. Nash Camp originally belonged to the founder of the Nash Motor Car Co., and Mr. Nash had a big-city decorator do his lodge.

It was a roomy lodge with plenty of room for guests, but the decorator made two mistakes: First, there was wall-to-wall white carpeting throughout, making it hard to clean. Second, there was no place to remove and hang waders, vest, creels, rods, and staffs. You either wore your waders inside, walking onto the white carpet, or took them off in the wet grass outside and then piled them on the white carpet inside.

Au Sable River Boats
Ernie once told me the story of the Au Sable longboats. They were originally built by the lumbermen to cruise the river, looking for timber stands. The Au Sable is a slow stream with gentle turns. The longboats are flat bottomed, typically twenty-four feet long, about four feet wide, and with about one foot of freeboard. They are easily controlled from the stern with a pole, and usually drag a few feet

of log chain so they coast a little slower than the current. There is a swivel seat in the bow for the angler, who can turn in the seat and easily step out to fish.

TU Founder George Griffith

Ernie and I once paid a courtesy call on George Griffith, who lived down on the Au Sable main branch. It was at George's house that Trout Unlimited was formed, and he was revered as a prime mover in the organization.

George had been discussing something with another guest, and he asked our opinion: Should he donate his autobiography to Trout Unlimited with the proviso that they work to put a stop to catch-and-release fishing? There had been a rather acrimonious battle to get those regulations, and by far the majority of fly anglers favored catch-and-release. George and his guest, however, did not.

I realized it was contentious, but I said I thought the proviso was not a good idea. George was much revered by anglers, and this would ruin the high regard in which he was held. George's guest cussed and stormed out, slamming the door behind him. I found out later he was the ringleader of the anti-no-kill group. George swallowed and said he guessed that was sound advice. Ernie supported me, and we ended up in harmony. The book, *For the Love of Trout*, was published in 1993.

The Bois Brule

In 1988 I visited the Bois Brule River in northwestern Wisconsin, and was curious about the origin of the name. Obviously French, it could still have different meanings. It could be a person's name or it could mean "burnt woods." The locals could not explain it, so I called Ernie.

"Well," Ernie explained, "in 1618 the French explorer Etienne Brulé was seeking a water route between the Great Lakes and the Mississippi. He paddled up many rivers, then finally the Brule, and found that the flowage that was the origin of the Brule was also the headwater of the St. Croix, which flows into the Mississippi." Who knew—except Ernie?

> # SEXUAL HARASSMENT
> # IS NOT A PROBLEM
> # AROUND HERE
>
> # IT'S A FRINGE BENEFIT

THE PC POLICE MADE THEM TAKE THIS DOWN.

Similar examples are innumerable. Years later I found that story in Ernie's *Trout*, almost word for word. Ernie had a prodigious memory. He swore it was not photographic, but it was close.

Lobster and Champagne

Ernie once told Carl and me of a fishing trip he took to New Zealand. After a few days, the party, which was ferried into the backcountry by helicopter, grew tired of eating the same fare and decided to have the helicopter bring them fresh lobster and cold Champagne from the coast. That pleased everyone, so they did it daily. Finally the trip's principle backer asked their guide how much this was costing them. The guide replied, "You don't want to know, mate. Just enjoy it while you still can. It's a long time looking up at the lid."

Who Is Buying the Wine?

A friend of Ernie's named Jack came into the shop one day and told me about a fishing trip he took with Ernie to Europe. Ernie invited him on the trip and said he would pay all expenses, provided Jack buy the wine. Jack said, "You have no idea what expensive wines Ernie could locate. I'm sure I spent more on the wine than he did on all the other expenses." I don't know how accurate that statement was, but it seems plausible.

■ ■ ■ ■ ■

Ernie loved to come back to Michigan, where he started his fishing career, and he got a kick out of a couple of my photos of signs. He favored "Sexual Harassment," which at that time hung over the bar at Ma Deeter's, and the one about the "low life thief" who stole the snow plow.

LOW LIFE THIEF WILL CALL SOON, YOU BET!

26 WHEN YOU CAN'T FISH, GO HUNTING

I got into hunting by way of Nancy's family. Her father, Glenn Stewart, took me rabbit hunting a couple of times, and I got interested. When I worked in Peoria we had some fairly good pheasant hunting in the cornfields. Unfortunately, he died just as we were beginning to enjoy our outings. I had looked forward to getting to do some more hunting with him, and maybe some fishing.

I inherited some of Glenn's guns. One of them, a Kentucky rifle, thrilled my grandson Jake. I decided Jake would give it a good home, so I gave it to him along with the Winchester '97 12-gauge that had belonged to his great-grandfather. Jake is now the fifth generation to hunt with that Winchester.

The family's hunting tradition goes back much further. They homesteaded in Illinois about 1830 near the first settlement that had not been massacred by Indian raiders. Everybody in the family worked—the men in the fields or at the mill or smithy, the women in the house and garden, the kids doing chores. Everybody, that is, except Milner. According to the family annals, "Brother Milner could not work like the others. He was rather poorly, and had erycipoleas [sic]of the ancle [sic]." Poor Milner had to spend all his time hunting and fishing, and "provided venison, turkey, rabbit, and other game,

IT IS EASIER TO TEACH A POINTER TO POINT THAN TO READ. BUT, HEY, WHAT'S THIS ABOUT NO DOGS?

plus fish from the bountiful streams." Was Milner slick or what?

Delmar Smith

A lot of anglers hunt as well as fish, so we carried hunting gear in our fly shop to satisfy their needs. Most anglers prefer hunting upland birds, but some get into waterfowl hunting, bow hunting, or some other variety of the sport.

Our longtime store manager, Wade Seley, arranged some dog-training programs. Wade got Delmar Smith, former dog trainer for Texas' King Ranch (the largest ranch in the United States) and a trainer of national champion field trial dogs, to teach some of them.

One of Delmar's most amazing techniques was to ask his students whether any of them had a problem dog. There were always plenty of them, and Delmar would say, "Bring 'er up. Now tell me what the problem is." It didn't matter what the problem was—Delmar would demonstrate how to solve it, usually within a few minutes. Then he'd have the owner do the same thing successfully.

Delmar told me the funniest thing he ever had happen in his classes occurred in a class for women. He asked them why they were taking the class, and one woman replied, "Well, every evening my husband comes in the front door, tosses his coat on the chair, goes out the back door, and pats the dog on the fanny. I figured I wanted some of that."

* * * * *

One of our friends had gone through Delmar's dog-training program. One day he came into the store ecstatic and told us about how beautifully his dog had done on a hunting trip out West. He showed me a great picture of his dog on point, which I admired. He said he had commissioned a painting of the picture, and hung it over the mantle in his living room. After a while he admitted his wife was not happy. She thought he ought to have her picture painted and put over the mantle.

I said, "I think you need to be more sensitive. After all, you got to take a week and go on that trip while she was stuck at home. But I think I know the perfect solution."

"What?" he asked.

"Tell her that when she can point like that, you will put the dog's picture in the den and put hers over the mantle."

Somehow, I don't imagine he suggested that to his wife.

No Flushing Dogs

Back in the late 1980s, a bunch of us decided to do some fall grouse hunting in northern Michigan. We rented a nice lodge and gathered a group of ten hunters. My pal Doug Truax, an author and publisher of hunting books, knew the territory best so I asked him to arrange for guides and dogs. "Pointing dogs, Doug, not flushing dogs," I said. We shared this preference, and he laughed.

Doug was the last to arrive at the lodge, while the rest of us were relaxing in the lobby. When he came in, I stage-whispered, "Got those pointing dogs, Doug? No flushers, right?"

"What's wrong with flushing dogs?" asked another pal, Andy Burrows from Chicago. Andy had been a lifelong English setter man but had recently changed to a springer spaniel. I made some sort of joke, but Andy was not amused. He was a longtime friend, so I tried to make amends by asking him if I could hunt with him.

The next day the hunting was terrible. When the group gathered that evening, I asked who got birds. Andy was the only hunter out of eight who got one—a bird that was located, flushed into shooting range, and retrieved perfectly by his springer. So I said, "OK, no more pointing dogs—its flushers from here on out!"

The next day was even worse. It was a beautiful day—sunny and windy—and no one got a bird. That's why I hate nice days! Then again, there have been some lousy days I hated, too.

Buster

Doug needed a new dog, so he went to the local animal shelter. There he found an English setter in terrible shape. He was about twenty pounds underweight and had a pellet wound in his chest. The feathering on his legs and tail was so worn that at first Doug thought he was a pointer. Still, Doug liked the dog and took him home. He named him Buster.

It took a couple of years and some hundreds of dollars to rejuvenate Buster. Even then he still had some problems. The dog feared running water and would not go near a stream. He would not even drink water from Doug's cupped hands when he could see the water had come from a stream.

One day Doug was hunting with a childhood friend named Dick. Doug shot a grouse that flew across the river before falling. Doug asked Dick to watch Buster since the dog would not cross the river. As Doug waded into the river, Buster followed all the way over and then back with him. Dick commented that the dog loved Doug more than he hated the water.

Doug and I hunted with Buster and the dog did a masterful job of finding and retrieving birds. It was a gamble that paid off equally for Doug and Buster.

Gypsy Joe

At bird-hunting camps, everyone has dog stories. I once had an English setter named Becky. The full name on her papers was Commander's Miss Becky. That dog was a running fool. She would take off in the field and be gone for as much as six hours before settling down to hunt. She would come into the house wagging her tail then in thirty seconds would be licking the windows, wanting to go outside. She slept on the pointed roof of her doghouse even when covered with snow. The kids on the school bus would cheer when Becky stood up and shook off the snow.

One year we went hunting for pheasants on a Michigan preserve to extend the season. I let Becky loose as soon as we got to the preserve. She took off immediately and topped three ridges before I lost sight of her. About 3:00 p.m. she returned and we got a few birds.

When we were through hunting, an old hillbilly caretaker came up to me and asked, "Hes thet bitch got any Gypsy Joe in 'er?"

I DON'T KNOW HOW THIS SOLD KNIVES, BUT THE BUSINESS IS IN THE THIRD GENERATION.

THIS MAY BE OVERKILL, BUT IT FITS THE TRADITION.

I didn't know what he was referring to and asked who Gypsy Joe was. The old man replied, "He was a big runnin' dog from down South. If she's got his blood, you'll never slow 'er down."

I checked Becky's pedigree papers when I got home. Sure enough, three generations back was Gypsy Joe! I soon traded her for some hunting privileges.

Jim Foote

Jim Foote was a world-champion carver of game birds and decoys, as well as a wildlife painter and printmaker. We carried his prints in our store.

Jim won the world carving championship with a carving of a pair of ruffed grouse. He sold the carving to Bubba Wood of Dallas, who had just opened a gallery called Collector's Covey. Bubba told Jim that he did not want to sell the carving, so he asked Jim to put a price on it that would ensure it did not sell. Jim suggested $15,000, and that was back in the 1980s.

Shortly after the grand opening of the gallery a customer named Charley called and said, "Bubba, I want them birds in your window."

"Why, Charley," Bubba exclaimed, "those birds cost $15,000!"

Charley replied, "I know. It just shows I got good taste. By the way, Bubba, what are them birds?"

■ ■ ■ ■ ■

Jim and a neighbor named Tom were avid duck hunters and carvers, and both collected decoys. Tom told me how they used to come off the marsh in the cold and burn Mason decoys to get warm. At the beginning of the twentieth century, Mason decoys were probably the best-selling decoys in the United States because they were inexpensive. Most of them were roughed out on a belt sander, which made them less expensive than carved decoys.

In 1905 premium-grade Mason decoys sold for $1. Today they are in great demand as collectibles. Some Masons now sell for up to $15,000. In January 2000 one Mason wood duck drake sold for the top price of $354,000, according to Russ Goldberger, an expert in antique decoys. I asked Russ how that price could have resulted and he assured me it was because the decoy was really rare, top grade, and in excellent condition. He said the same decoy would now sell for a good deal more.

■ ■ ■ ■

Jim Foote once told me he would take me grouse hunting if I took him trout fishing. While we were fishing, he took some pictures, one of which he turned into a painting. It showed me fishing from the bow seat of one of the classic Au Sable longboats, being poled by a guide named Greg.

Jim gave me a print, titled *Autumn Float*. I thanked him, especially for painting out my bald spot. Nancy asked him, "What if it doesn't sell?"

". . . I'll paint back the bald spot," Jim quipped.

Autumn Float by Jim Foote

"If it doesn't sell, I'll paint back the bald spot."—Jim Foote

27 GO WEST, OLD MAN

The Bucket List

At the age of seventy-seven I decided to make a "bucket list," a list of the places I wanted to fish before I got too old or kicked the bucket. I have fished extensively in Europe, especially on England's premier chalk streams, the Test and Itchen. And I fished lots of great Michigan rivers in forty-plus years of fly fishing.

My Rocky Mountain trips included fishing many rivers in Colorado, Montana, Wyoming, and a few other states. I had fished at least a dozen rivers around Yellowstone National Park but had never fished in it. Most of my Rocky Mountain trips were business related so I fished with dealers or clients outside the park.

Every time I started working on the bucket list Yellowstone became the obvious first choice. Many of my friends and customers had told me great stories about the fabulous streams, the unbelievable wildlife, and the eye-popping scenery. The park is the origin of many of the important western fishing rivers—including the Yellowstone, Madison, Gallatin, Shoshone, and Snake, which includes both the South Fork and the Henry's Fork—and so provides a variety of river types and fishing. I didn't even get to a second choice on the list. I discussed it with my fishing companion, Dick Smith, and we decided to go.

Yellowstone National Park is the source of
most of the Rocky Mountain rivers.

■ ■ ■ ■ ■

In September 2009 Dick and I flew to Billings and rented a minivan, an ideal vehicle for two anglers, then got on the road. The first day was devoted to travel and sightseeing. The map showed Beartooth Pass as an exceptionally twisted road, and it was. We drove sixty-four miles of road to cover a distance of eight miles as the crow flies. Charles Kuralt is said to have called this the country's most beautiful highway, but it was snowing so hard we couldn't see it. The constant hairpin turns at 11,000 feet were slippery and we were mostly concerned with getting to a lower altitude below the snow.

After the pass, we started down Chief Joseph Scenic Highway toward Cody. I had read that Kuralt also called this one the country's most beautiful roads. It is spectacular. The scenery is composed of the most varied eye-catching rock formations I have ever seen, and ponds with wading moose feeding in the waterweeds.

Dick and I stopped at the Buffalo Bill Historical Center in Cody, a remarkable collection of displays of western art, artifacts, and guns. You could easily spend several hours there looking at paintings and sculptures by Remington and Russell, and studying the extensive display of weapons including the old Colt six-shooters and Winchester repeating rifles that played such an important part in the history of the West.

The Henry's Fork

The Yellowstone and Madison were reportedly not fishing well so Dick and I took a day to try the Henry's Fork of the Snake. We got advice from Three Rivers Ranch in Idaho on where to fish at the Railroad Ranch in Harriman State Park.

It was not a good time to be fishing the Henry's Fork, but we did pretty well for a few hours. I had wanted Dick to see the river, which I have seen boiling with good fish in the proper season. It has the reputation of being the most challenging of rivers due to the great variety and quantity of flies hatching. Our time there mainly whetted our appetite for a possible future trip.

The Henry's Fork runs through a large, flat valley with the dramatically jagged Teton Range to the east. Once you have seen the Tetons' profile, you will always recognize it. It looks the same from the east and north of Jackson Hole. You can enjoy the silhouette of this range from the Jackson side in the evening and from the Idaho side in the morning.

The Firehole River

The Firehole River is located near the town of West Yellowstone. The weather was cold around there, but the Firehole is warmed by hot springs that bubble out of the river and the surrounding land.

We had fair fishing for a couple of hours in the morning. Anglers will appreciate a tough fishing challenge and we found it there in the afternoon. Fish were rising constantly, but we could not get them to take our flies. We knew they were supposed to be taking blue-winged olives, but we had good drifts over feeding fish time after time without a single take. Then we found the reason: The olives the fish were taking were size #28, and the smallest we had were #24. That is small, but not small enough.

I will never forget a trio of otters that spied me from a distance and then swam closer and closer. They surfaced constantly to look at me, finally getting within about twenty feet. They seemed curious about how a fellow fisherman was faring.

Our guide, Tom Travis, was an old friend of mine. Tom has long been a leading expert, guide, entomologist, and lecturer. I always spend a good deal of time discussing fishing with Tom, and always find wisdom in his observations. I consider us fortunate to have had him as a guide on this trip.

Chico Hot Springs

Dick and I decided to make Chico our headquarters and move to the northern section of the park, as the reports were best there. Chico is an old spa that was started around 1840 near Emigrant, Montana. The main hotel is about a hundred years old. The lobby and the dining

THE FIREHOLE IS STEAMIN'!

MY BEST BROWN FROM DEPUY'S.

room have a lot of charm, but the rooms are small and the bathroom facilities are Spartan. If you crave comfort you go to the newer units, but they were full during our visit. The bar seems to be hopping all the time.

Chico is north of the park, halfway to Livingston. It is convenient to both the spring creeks of Paradise Valley and the northeastern rivers of the park.

DePuy's Spring Creek

DePuy's is a world-class spring creek that adjoins Armstrong's Spring Creek. I have fished both creeks several times and have always been thrilled by them. The spring waters are warm enough to fish year-round and provide several miles of seldom easy and always challenging fishing.

Dick had never been there and he managed to have a great day. I caught fewer fish than he did, but got my best trout of the trip, a hefty brown. DePuy's started our best run of luck, which continued for the rest of the trip.

The Lamar River and Tributary Soda Butte Creek

The Yellowstone Valley is impressive for its deep gorges and waterfalls. In contrast, the Lamar Valley is wide and flat. It contains long vistas of grazing areas for the wildlife. We would see herds of buffalo, antelope, elk, and mule deer every evening. At times we would have to stop the car to let the buffalo pass.

Soda Butte Creek is named for a mineral formation formed by an old hot spring. Until the last day, it was my favorite stream in the park. We could almost always find good fish, and seldom had more than an hour go by without catching one. Soda Butte is a tributary of the Lamar. There is a footbridge across Soda Butte on the Lamar Trail, and the pool under that bridge constantly showed good cutthroat trout feeding.

Dick and I worked back and forth between the Lamar and Soda Butte over three days, all on dry flies. In fact, I never even tied on anything but a dry fly. All I remember is we caught a lot of cutthroat. In September you do not see many huge fish, but most were between sixteen and twenty inches and they provided excellent action. Our days were generally sunny, but I have learned you do not fish in the Rockies without having a rain jacket at hand. A sunny day can turn rainy in minutes. Several days did, then the skies cleared just as fast.

Slough Creek

Throughout this trip Tom Travis, our guide, had urged us to keep an eye out for a green drake hatch. He thought we might find them on Slough Creek. I have some experience with the western green drakes. During the summer, I had caught a seven-pound rainbow on a dry green drake in Colorado. In September we were expecting not only a different species, but a different genus as well, *Timpanoga hecuba*. Fortunately, it fished just like the green drakes I was familiar with.

The green drake is a large insect that hatches around the middle of the day. Its size and the fact that it hatches in great numbers causes the best fish to attack the drakes with vigor, showing their backs out of the water to get them. The only downside of such hatches is that the natural insects are so numerous that it is sometimes hard to get fish to take an artificial.

That day on Slough Creek, the fish were taking. We had rising trout for a couple of hours. Dick took the best fish, over twenty inches, and we ended the fishing well satisfied.

* * * * *

We drove to Billings after dark and got a comfortable rest with a nice shower.

Next morning, as we headed to the airport, Dick spotted a sign to the famous Boot Hill Cemetery, so named because its residents died with their boots on. We drove to the hill, and it occurred to me that this was a warning to get back to work on my bucket list.

SLOUGH CREEK

He can have his grass if I can have my pool.

28 I'LL BE ZERNED

Ed Zern was a renowned outdoors humorist. Paul Schullery, in his book *The History of American Fly Fishing*, called Ed the most important outdoors humorist of the twentieth century. He was known especially for his monthly column in *Field & Stream* magazine, "Exit Laughing." Ed was a modest, friendly soul. He amused people and he knew it, but he was content to fit in with the group. I knew him to take the stage but not to upstage anyone else. Gray hair and rumpled clothes seemed right on Ed.

Sometime in the late 1980s, Carl Richards and I, along with a group of friends, had the occasion to take Ed on a fishing trip to the Pere Marquette. The river is one of Michigan's better trout streams, with a wealth of fishing lore. It was the location of the first successful planting of brown trout in the United States, and was the subject of a memorable chapter in Ernie Schwiebert's *Remembrances of Rivers Past*. It was also the home stream of Justin and Fannie Leonard, who wrote *Mayflies of Michigan Trout Streams*, a scientific work much respected because of its sound entomology and early use of color photographs.

Carl and I drove with Ed to Barothy Lodge, where we had rented one of their chalets, which are about as pretty as you can find. They are roomy and rustic, with room for maybe a dozen guys. They each have a large lounging room, a big stone fireplace, and window walls three stories high. That night we were treated to the spectacle of flying squirrels diving down from the roof to bird feeders on the porch under floodlights. The next morning there were wild turkeys at the feeders.

To be on the banks of this fabled stream with Ed Zern was a memorable event in my fishing life. We stayed up all night talking about our favorite Zern stories, stumbling to bed after Ed fell asleep on the couch, about 7:00 a.m. None of us was worth a hoot on the stream that afternoon, but none of us would have changed a thing.

My favorite of Ed's works is his book *Hunting and Fishing from A to Zern*. Following are a few selections.

■ ■ ■ ■ ■

Older readers will remember that *Lady Chatterly's Lover* was about Lady Chatterly and her affair with her husband's gamekeeper. Ed put a different spin on it:

BOOK REVIEW

Although written many years ago, *Lady Chatterly's Lover* has just been reissued by Grove Press, and this fictional account of the day-to-day life of an English gamekeeper is still of considerable interest to outdoor minded readers, as it contains many passages on pheasant raising, the apprehending of poachers, ways of controlling vermin, and other chores and duties of the professional gamekeeper. Unfortunately one is obliged to wade through many pages of extraneous material in order to discover and savor these sidelights on the management of a Midland shooting estate, and in this reviewer's opinion this book can not take the place of J. R. Miller's *Practical Gamekeeping*.

■ ■ ■ ■ ■

Ed claimed that anglers might at times be careless with the truth, and thought that was justified because "I get all the truth I need in the newspaper every morning, and every chance I get I go fishing, or swap stories with fishermen, to get the taste of it out of my mouth."

■ ■ ■ ■ ■

Ed wrote of the beginning fly fisherman who made great progress learning to cast, using the 10 o'clock to 2 o'clock technique, which cautioned the caster not to let his rod drift past those points. The poor guy nearly had a nervous breakdown when daylight saving time began. I guess he couldn't decide whether to make it 9 o'clock to 1 o'clock or 11 o'clock to 3 o'clock.

■ ■ ■ ■ ■

My favorite Zernism:

HARD QUESTIONS ANSWERED

Q: When I became engaged, my fiancée said she understood how much I loved to hunt and fish, and promised never to interfere. Now we're married, and she nags me night and day to give up outdoor sports altogether. She says if I loved her I'd gladly stay home. If this keeps up I'm going to blow my brains out. Please give me whatever advice you can. J.R.Y., Akron Ohio.

A: Since trajectory isn't important here, our recommendation would be a .35 Remington with 200-grain soft-nose bullet. E.Z.

■ ■ ■ ■ ■

One last zinger of Ed's: "It is widely supposed that Jonah exited the whale the same way he entered—but that is purely suppository."

■ ■ ■ ■ ■

Ed died in March 1994 at age eighty-three. I'd like to think he exited laughing.

I DARE SAY.

EPILOGUE: The Trout Stream

Arriving at the trout stream and spending the day there is one of the most pleasurable experiences possible. We anglers are among the fortunate few because we have found one way to be happy. Many people have showed us, helped us, and taught us, and we owe them our gratitude.

John Voelker loved the challenge of fishing, and so do we. Carl Richards found the mystery of fly hatches endlessly intriguing, and so do some of us. Nick Lyons greatly enjoyed nature's surroundings, but never lost sight of the fact that he was there to catch fish. A few anglers love just being on the stream, maybe enjoying a lunch or basking in the sunshine. Certainly there is no lovelier place to be.

I have finally concluded that spending a day on the stream is one of the major joys of life. The other is arriving home at the end of the day to love, friendship, and comfort.

After forty years of trout fishing, I have never run out of new questions and puzzles to solve. I think any good hobby requires that constant mystery. You can never be a perfect angler, nor golfer, nor chess master, nor bridge player. There are enough quandaries to keep you searching as long and as far as you choose. Angling is a science that is never exhausted.

THE TROUT STREAM.